More praise for *This Party's Got to Stop*:

'This extraordinary memoir, ᴏ᷄ recent years, charts the existen one's parents and the persisting remain between the siblings v longing here to make the heart w ᴏᴜᴛ ᴛʜᴇʳᴇ is beauty and love and tenderness too. Every paragraph is an exquisite object' Hisham Matar

'A terrific memoir of grief and loss at the death of two parents, shot through with moments of black comedy' *Scotland on Sunday*

'A book about how the dead continue to influence the living, and how grief can warp into madness . . . *This Party's Got to Stop* has the unsettling combination of very precise, often witty prose applied to deep pain, like fine stitches applied, over and over again, to a wound, that, despite everything, remains wide open' *Daily Mail*

'Spikily funny and very dark. It's also a beautifully constructed book. Each chapter has the form of a short story, the whole has the drive of a novel, and yet what we're told – the loss of a mother, the loss of a father, a group of siblings drawn back together by death, before springing drastically apart – has the affidavit force of a memoir, of lived experience. The result is singular, like everything Rupert Thomson does. I greatly admire his generic unruliness, or rather restlessness, which is clearly a function of his perfectionism as a writer' Robert Macfarlane

'Thomson neatly captures the way your family background seems both stranger and more important as the years pass. He writes with a winning kindliness that never turns soppy' *Daily Telegraph*

'This walk through a family's buried shadows continually takes the reader by surprise' *Metro*

'Thomson's moving portrait of three young brothers struggling with the death of their parents explores the true complexity of family; the way in which ties are bound more tightly and intensely by loss, messy grudges and separation' *Big Issue*

'What a joy it is to read an autobiography where the hype is wholly justified' *Bookseller*

'Very funny. Rupert Thomson is such an attentive writer, and the quality of his attention brings the smallest incidents to life' Hilary Mantel

'Emotionally honest and genuinely affecting' *Economist*

'Thomson is incapable of writing a dull sentence and he brilliantly captures the contradictory nature of his father and how young men deal, or refuse to deal, with grief' *Irish Sunday Independent*

'An intriguingly unconventional memoir' *TLS*

'A moving, honest and funny tragedy' *Esquire*

'Elegant, beautifully observed and captivatingly atmospheric' *Marie Claire*

'Moving, darkly humorous' *List*

'This memoir combines charm, sharpness and high emotion to devastating effect' *Waterstone's Books Quarterly*

THIS PARTY'S GOT TO STOP

RUPERT THOMSON

A MEMOIR

GRANTA

Granta Publications, 12 Addison Avenue, London W11 4QR

First published in Great Britain by Granta Books, 2010
This paperback edition published by Granta Books, 2011

A CIP catalogue record for this book
is available from the British Library.

1 3 5 7 9 10 8 6 4 2

ISBN 978 1 84708 174 2

Typeset by M Rules

Printed and bound in Great Britain
by CPI Bookmarque, Croydon

Mixed Sources
Product group from well-managed
forests and other controlled sources
www.fsc.org Cert no. TT-COC-002227
© 1996 Forest Stewardship Council
FSC

To Peter Straus

1965

My mother spoke to me once after she was dead. Nine years old, I was standing outside our house, in the shadow of a yew tree, when I heard her call my name. It came from high up, and to my left, and I imagined for a moment that she was upstairs, but all the windows at the front of the house were closed, and there was nothing pale in any of those black rectangles, nothing to suggest a face. Besides, I felt her voice had come from outside. Real and clear, but disembodied, like a recording – though later I thought it was how an angel might sound, if an angel were to speak. I stared at the yew tree – its splintered bark, its scratchy leaves – and noticed how dull the berries looked, their red skin covered with a milky bloom. I stared at the scuffed toes of my shoes. I had answered my mother's call – I had said, 'Yes?' – but I heard nothing else, and my one simple monosyllable hung in the silence of that summer afternoon until it seemed I had been talking to myself.

*

My mother had died suddenly the year before, aged thirty-three. My brother, Robin, and I were at school that day. We went to lessons. We had lunch. We didn't know.

When school finished, we walked home, which took half an hour. It was hot, even for July, and I could smell grass cuttings and the tar melting at the edge of the road. Three years younger than me, and something of a dreamer, Robin lagged behind as usual, and I arrived at the house ahead of him, but stopped as soon as I turned in through the gate. My uncle's Jaguar was parked in front of our garage. I glanced back down the hill. Robin was still a hundred yards away, socks around his ankles, cap askew. He looked exhausted and fed up – the long walk home was the part of the day he dreaded most – but when I shouted that Uncle Roland had come to visit, his face brightened and he speeded up.

I waited until he reached the gate, then we both ran up the drive. The back door was open. The house felt cool. Through the kitchen, across the hall. On into the sitting-room. Then darkness suddenly, and silence. I seem to remember shadowy figures at the edges of the room. I don't remember what was said.

I bent over my bed, my face in my hands, my body shaking. Crying kept what had happened at a distance, stopped it becoming real. Crying meant I didn't have to believe it. The counterpane was cream-coloured, with delicate orange stitching, and smelled as if it had just been washed. Granny Dickie – my father's mother – stood behind me. I felt her hand on the back of my head. She said my name, and then she said I was going to have to be brave.

I spoke into the counterpane. 'I don't want to be brave.'

'I know, darling.'

I imagine she stared past me, towards the bedroom window. Outside, the weather was beautiful. My face stung.

'I know,' she said again.

I turned and pressed myself against her skirt, still trying not to see or understand. Our front garden lay in shadow, but intense orange sunlight coloured the tops of the trees and the roof of the house over the road, as if that half of the view had been dipped in a sweet syrup.

The seventh of July. Long days.

I often tell people I can't remember anything before I was eight, but it's not true. I remember lying on the back seat of a car during a thunderstorm, the sky folding and crumpling above me – I was still a baby then – and I remember being two or three and watching bits of a cup dart across the kitchen floor while my parents shouted overhead. I remember being five and falling for a girl called Rowena. What I can't remember is my mother. Her sudden death wiped her out, like a teacher rubbing chalk words off a blackboard. I can remember a dress she used to wear – pink with white polka-dots – but somehow she isn't there inside it. I can't remember her legs, or her shoulders. I can't remember what shape her fingernails were. I think I can remember the smell of her lipstick, but I can't see her mouth. I can't remember how she sounded, even though I heard her call me once when she was dead. Was her voice light and breathy, or was it deep? Did she have an accent? I have no idea. I try and remember her saying the ordinary things that mothers are always saying to their children, things she must have said thousands of times during the eight years we were together. *Hello. Come here. I love you.*

But no, nothing.

*

Not long after her death, I left school in the middle of the day. On the street, it was unusually quiet; the sun lit a world that seemed motionless, suspended, like a statue of itself. I came down out of Meads village and turned along Link Road. Deciding not to cross the golf course, which was the short-cut home, I started up Paradise Drive. The woods rose ahead of me, the foliage massed in brooding clusters like a mushroom cloud.

The pavement narrowed and then vanished altogether, and I had no choice but to walk on the road. The bend into the trees was deceptively sharp; if any cars came the other way, they wouldn't see me until the last moment. Dad was always saying people drove too fast on Paradise Drive. It was a miracle, he would say, that nobody had been run over.

I shivered as the shade of the woods closed over me. Through the trees I could see the golf course, its fairways smooth in the sunlight. On top of the greenness was a narrow strip of blue. The sea.

When I reached our house, Dad was sitting at the far end of the kitchen table, a spoon halfway to his mouth. In the bowl in front of him was his favourite pudding – stewed blackcurrants and custard. He looked at me as if I were a stranger. 'What are *you* doing here?'

'I've come home,' I said.

'But it's only lunchtime.'

He must have heard my footsteps, wondered who it was. He wouldn't have been expecting anyone to walk in through the back door, not at that time of day, and not without knocking first or calling out. Did he think for a moment that it was his wife returning, even though he had watched her coffin drop into the ground? Was that why he had seemed so shocked, and why his voice had sounded different? Perhaps it had been in his mind to say, You're back, or, My darling. Then I appeared.

What are you *doing here?*

Normally, when school was over, Robin and I would catch a bus to the Town Hall and then walk home, but I hadn't thought to query the sun's position or the fact that I was on my own. Everything felt automatic, and harmonious. It felt *right*. I wonder whether, at some deep level, I had been trying to out-manoeuvre fate. I had learned that bad things happened when I wasn't there. If I made my absences more unpredictable, the bad things would be less likely to occur. Or perhaps – just perhaps – in taking the route that was longer and more hazardous, I was risking some kind of misadventure. I missed my mother. I longed for her. I wanted to follow her, to go where she had gone . . .

The deceptive bend, the speeding cars.

The cool shadow of the wood.

Perhaps it wasn't the thought of his wife walking in through the back door that had startled my father. Perhaps it was something he saw in my face.

Sorry If I Look Strange

A Wednesday morning, twenty years later. I lie in bed and stare out of the window. A thin crust of snow clings to the tiled rooftops, and the sky beyond is grey, a Berlin grey, steely and unrelenting. I glance at the clock. Half past eight. Soon Hanne will be off to work, a drug rehab unit near the border. I met Hanne the previous summer, on the Amalfi coast. Her slim, tanned legs, her face as mobile as a clown's. Her easy laughter. We lived in Hamburg to start with, then she got a job in West Berlin. Tomorrow it's her birthday. She'll be thirty-one.

Only minutes after Hanne has left the apartment, the phone rings next to the bed.

'Rupert?'

It's Robin. Since leaving art college, Robin has moved into my old council flat in London. Neither of us has much money, so we rarely speak to each other on the phone. It must be important, I think, for him to be calling me like this.

'Dad's in hospital,' he says. 'He's having trouble breathing.'

My heart lurches. 'I'll fly over.'

'You don't need to. They told me he wasn't – what's that word they use? – he wasn't critical.'

'I'll come anyway.'

The last time I saw my father I lied to him. Three months have passed since then, and I still feel bad about it.

'Where are you?' I ask.

'In Eastbourne. At the house.'

He says that when he rang Dad the other day, the au pair answered. She told him Dad had been taken to Midhurst. She had been alone for two days, and had heard nothing. She sounded anxious, bewildered. I remember a short, shy girl with light brown hair. I remember, too, that Dad thinks she's a bit dull, and that he has given her the nickname 'Forbes'.

He's having trouble breathing.

During the war, my father served in the North Atlantic, first on destroyers, then on motor-torpedo boats, but in 1943, at the age of twenty-one, he caught pneumonia. Both lungs were affected. He spent the next ten years in hospital, and was subjected to several major operations. He has always dreaded having to go back. Even his six-monthly check-ups frighten him. If a hospital ever appears on TV, he switches channels.

That night, Hanne and I sit at our living-room table, drinking wine. Our apartment is on the ground floor, and looks directly on to one of Kreuzberg's smaller streets. Outside, people are walking home from work, their features smudged by the sheet of rose-coloured plastic Hanne has fastened to the bottom half of the window. We talk about Dad, whom she has never met. When I saw him in November, he made it clear that he didn't understand my relationship with Hanne, and could see no future in it, and I flew back to West Berlin feeling aggrieved, but when I suggested to her that perhaps we should have nothing to do with him for a while, she disagreed. Her mother was always saying such things, she told me. Hanne thought it best simply to ignore his disapproval. Tonight, though, she wonders what would happen if I took her to England with me. Would he like her?

'Maybe,' I say. 'If he could get over his prejudice.'

'What is prejudice?'

I explain.

'Oh yes,' she says. 'Yes, I know. Nobody likes the fucking Germans.'

I touch her face. 'I do.'

The next morning Hanne leaves for work at eight-thirty, as usual, even though it's her birthday. We will celebrate later on, when she comes home. Since I have just received my unemployment benefit, a sum of about 600 marks, I'm thinking of taking her to Exil, a fashionable restaurant on the Paul-Lincke-Ufer, but the phone rings and changes everything.

Robin says my name. Then he says, 'Dad's dead.'

'Jesus,' I say. 'God.'

Outside, in the courtyard, an old woman watches as her dog cocks its leg against the back wheel of a bicycle. Her coat is the waterlogged dark green of a rotten kiwi fruit. I glance at the clock. Five past nine. Something about the angle of the hands seems grotesque. It makes me feel dizzy, as though I'm standing next to a big drop, and I wonder if I'm going to be sick.

'Jesus,' I say again.

My lips feel clumsy, numb.

Robin tells me that Dad died in the night. The cause of death was respiratory failure.

'That's what he was always scared of,' I say. 'Not being able to breathe.'

'They told me it was peaceful.'

Peaceful? I don't see how that can be true. I'm not even sure what it means.

'Did you visit him?' I ask.

'No.' A woman at the hospital said he could wait until the weekend. She told him not to worry. 'So I didn't worry,' Robin says bitterly, 'and now he's dead.' He talked to Dad, though, on the phone. He asked Dad how he felt, and was startled by the vehemence of the reply. *How do you* think *I feel?* He had never heard Dad say anything quite so abrasive. 'He was almost sarcastic,' Robin tells me. He was also surprised by Dad's voice, which sounded harsh and gravelly. 'I should have known,' he says.

'At least you spoke to him,' I say. 'At least one of us called.'

Why didn't I think of picking up the phone?

'They asked if I wanted to view the body.' Robin laughs nervously. 'I'm not sure I want to.'

'Well, I do.' More than a thousand miles separate me from my father, and I have to try and close the gap. Close it to an inch or two. My mouth to his ear. My hand on his heart. 'You don't have to go. I'll drive over by myself.'

Robin doesn't say anything.

'Have you spoken to Ralph?' I ask. Ralph is our other brother – the youngest of the three.

'Not yet.'

When Robin hangs up forty minutes later, my sense of isolation is so immediate and profound that it registers as a drop in the temperature, and I begin to shake with cold.

Why didn't I ring Dad? I didn't have the number of the hospital, but I could have asked Robin for it, or called Directory Enquiries. I was Dad's eldest son. He would have found it comforting to hear my voice. I could have let him know I was on my way. I could have told him I loved him. But now, all of a sudden, it's too late. Though I'm in bed, with the duvet drawn up to my chin, I'm still trembling. My legs appear to have no feeling in them. They're smooth and dry; they might be made of wood. Before we moved into our apartment, it was a print studio. The room we sleep in used to be the darkroom. It took coat after coat of white paint to obliterate the black, but as I stare up at the ceiling I can sense its presence, like a shadow pressing from beneath.

I call Hanne and tell her what has happened. She puts me on hold while she goes to ask Ernst, her team leader, for permission to leave early.

'The bastard,' she mutters when she returns.

'What did he say?'

'He said the day ends at five o'clock.'

I tell her I need to fly to England as soon as possible. There's a travel agent round the corner, she says. On Kottbusser Damm. In the background, I can hear one of the junkies' babies screaming.

'I'm not sure I can do this on my own,' I say.

'You can,' she says. 'I know you can.'

She promises to be home by six.

I wash and dress. Grey light filters through panes of frosted glass. Toothpaste. The mirror. A pair of boots.

Things seem mundane, precarious. The world, like a bowl filled to the brim with water, is something that can be dropped or spilled. I leave the apartment. Old snow has been shovelled into long uneven ridges at the edges of the cobbled pavement. The air smells of coal. Outside the shop that sells electrical appliances is the usual cluster of middle-aged Turkish men in leather jackets. It's so cold that everyone has tears in their eyes; when I push through the door of the travel agency, no one suspects that I've been crying.

In stumbling German, I tell the woman behind the desk that I need to fly to London urgently. Tomorrow, if possible. Only scheduled flights are available at such short notice, she says. It will be expensive. Her eyelids are the blue of blackbirds' eggs. Her hair is glossy, wire-stiff. I tell her that I have no choice. There's been a death in the family. As I speak, I have a sense not of an echo exactly but of a kind of superimposition – how many times, I wonder, have people come out with that sentence? – and the effect is both prolonged and underlined as the woman solemnly lifts her eyes to mine and says she's sorry. I end up spending my entire dole cheque on a British Airways flight to Gatwick.

Walking back to the apartment, I realize that the life I have been living for the past fifteen months – first in Tuscany, and now here, in West Berlin – is being brushed aside, and I am doing nothing to prevent that happening. I suppose I have always known this moment would arrive. Even as a boy, I was afraid my Dad would die – but he didn't, and he didn't, and I began, little by little, to trust him, to believe that he could last. How perverse that his death should come only when I've got out of the habit of expecting it!

I turn the corner into Sanderstrasse, and as I pass the cake-shop with its old-fashioned brown-and-gold lettering I am briefly wrapped in the bitter, sumptuous fragrance of dark chocolate. My fingers tighten round the one-way ticket in the pocket of my coat. I feel as if something has been achieved. I also, oddly, feel less alone.

Three months ago, I caught a train to Eastbourne, the town where I had grown up and where my father still lived. I arrived later than intended, and there were no lights on in the house when the taxi pulled up outside. I knocked on the front door. Nobody answered. I walked round to the back and stood on the lawn. The cherry trees that grew on the south side of the garden stirred in the night air. Nearby was the sycamore I used to climb when I was young. Dad's bedroom window was dark, the curtains drawn; in the moonlight, the glasshouse appeared to be built from sheets of ice. I called his name. Softly, though. As if afraid I might rouse him. To disturb Dad was to break one of the rules that had governed my childhood. When he had finished lunch and swallowed his pills, he would go upstairs, and my two brothers and I would have to be quiet for the next hour and a half, but we were boys, and as we tiptoed from room to room, talking in exaggerated whispers, one of us would invariably knock a chair over or let a door slam shut. Even the chink of a spoon against the lip of a cup could be fatal. *You woke me up.* How often had we heard those words? I felt guilty every time – and not just of carelessness or disobedience: in depriving Dad of his much-needed rest, we were affecting his chances of survival.

I picked up a chunk of dry mud from the flower bed and

flung it at his window. It fell back, landing on the glass-house roof and almost shattering a pane. Dad's curtains didn't move. He must already have taken his Seconal. I swore under my breath, then walked round to the front door again. This time I held the letter box open and put my mouth to the gap.

'Dad? Dad!'

I must have called his name thirty times.

At last I heard the click of his bedroom door. I watched one-eyed through the upright letter box as he felt his way down the stairs in his tartan dressing-gown, then I let the flap close quietly and stood back.

When he opened the door, he had a curious, almost absent-minded smile on his face, and his hair was adrift on the top of his head, wispy and unkempt.

'Sorry if I look strange,' he said.

I stepped forwards and wrapped my arms around him. It was like hugging a basket of eggs, you had to be so careful.

'I'm sorry I'm late,' I said. 'I missed my train.'

'I was fast asleep. Dead out.'

'You go back to bed, Dad. I'm in now.'

At breakfast I apologized again.

'All the years go by,' he said, 'but you never forget the sound of your child calling you in the middle of the night . . .'

Later, he talked for half an hour without a break – about the new poems he had written, about a plan to end his days in a retired sailors' home near Portsmouth and, lowering his voice, about Forbes.

At last he sat back in his red chair, saying his throat hurt. He took a sip of water, then stared out into the room. 'Now you tell me something.'

But I could hardly talk about my time in London – any mention of nightclubs or parties left him baffled, even vexed – and though I had told him, in my letters, about my move to West Berlin, I doubted he would want to hear about that either. He blamed the war for robbing him of both his youth and his health, and was unlikely to approve of my involvement with a German girl; he might even think I'd done it on purpose, to upset him. Dad had his own ambitions for me. His grandmother had been Scottish – a Johnston – and several years of genealogical research had revealed a branch of the family that had once owned vast tracts of land in Dumfriesshire. He believed it was my duty, as his eldest son, to make money and buy them back. He also wanted me to claim a title – Marquis of Annandale – and a clan leadership, both of which, he argued, were rightfully ours. When I took a job as a copywriter in London in 1978, Dad thought this was a move in the right direction, but my resignation four years later mystified and disappointed him, and he was always trying to persuade me to reconsider. Since he was a poet himself, albeit an unpublished one, surely he ought to have understood when I told him that my intention was to write, but in a recent letter, posted on 23 October, he suggested that I look for advertising work in West Berlin – 'to keep my hand in', as he put it. To my father, a career in advertising signified security, wealth, even glamour; above all, though, it was a stepping-stone to the life he had mapped out for me.

Later that day, I handed him a Polaroid of Hanne, which I had taken on the steps of a Tuscan church the previous summer. He held the photo at arm's length, a habit he'd acquired since his eyesight started going, and one he tended to exaggerate. Eventually, he asked why I was wearing such peculiar clothes. At first I didn't follow. Then I had to laugh.

'That's not *me*, Dad. That's *her*.'

He shook his head and leaned back in his chair, staring up into the corner of the room.

I took the picture from him and studied it closely. Hanne was nearly as tall as I was, and we both had dark brown hair, but could she honestly be mistaken for me? Surely not. In the end, I thought his misreading of the Polaroid was a refusal to acknowledge her existence. He didn't see her because he didn't *want* to see her.

At the beginning of my visit, I had told him I would be leaving on Monday morning, but on Sunday night, while we were standing next to each other in the scullery, doing the washing-up, he turned to me. 'Can't you stay a bit longer?'

'Not really,' I said. 'My flight's on Tuesday.'

It wasn't true. I wasn't flying back until the end of the week, but I wanted to be in London, with my friends.

Dad looked down at the draining-board, lips pressed together. 'We didn't have much time, did we?'

After my visit to the travel agent, I stay indoors. Only two colours register: the white of the snow spread thinly on the rooftops, and the red of the living-room carpet. Sitting on the floor, arms wrapped round my knees, I play the same record over and over until it becomes the soundtrack for my father's death. I can't seem to break out of the state into which I descended the moment my phone call with Robin finished. That instant, blanket desolation.

At last, a key turns in the lock, and Hanne appears in the living-room doorway.

'I'm sorry about your birthday,' I say.

Kneeling, she puts her arms around me. Her leather jacket is so icy that I shiver; she has brought the cold air in with her. Though she holds me tight, I can't find it in myself to respond, or even to alter the position of my body.

Later, she sits on a chair by the wall. One leg drawn up against her chest, she watches me. 'It's like there's something over you,' she says. 'I can't get near you.'

But I don't feel enclosed, or sealed off. I feel as if I've shrunk. I feel *small*. There seems to be less of me than there was before, and I wonder what it is I've lost.

Apart from a father, that is.

The following day, Hanne drives me to the airport. I can't stop yawning. We didn't go out to celebrate, as planned. Instead, we lit candles and opened a bottle of red wine. We sat in the living-room, our voices hushed, the plate-glass window creaking with the cold. I told Hanne how brisk Robin had sounded on the phone, almost officious; I'd barely recognized him. She imagined it would have been a shock for him to find out his father was in hospital. He'd be running on pure adrenaline. As for Ralph, I said, the last time I had spoken to him was three years ago, at his wedding. What would it be like when *he* arrived? How would we all get on?

'Maybe it's a chance to be closer,' Hanne said.

'I don't know,' I said. 'Maybe.'

We stayed up till four.

I stare at the beautiful, dilapidated streets. Buildings the colour of smoke. Graffiti, bullet holes. Canals. I will miss Berlin, but it feels superseded, beside the point. I'm like an actor who has been standing in the footlights, only to discover that the real play is happening off-stage.

Hanne asks how long I will be gone.

'I don't know,' I say. 'I've no idea.'

Though I sense her eyes on me, there's nothing I can tell her that will be of any comfort. She's in the car with me, only inches away, but like the city she has begun to seem superfluous, irrelevant.

At check-in, the stewardess says I'm only allowed one item of hand baggage. Every word I have written since I walked out of advertising has been written on my portable, a maroon Olympia with art deco curves and chrome trim, but since I have packed a camera in my holdall, I let her take the typewriter.

As Hanne and I drink a last coffee together, she glances at her watch. 'You must hurry, or you'll miss your fly.'

I can't help smiling.

'What?' she says.

Hanne's English is like nobody else's. Once, while describing a camping trip, she said that her tent had flooded and her dreaming packet had nearly floated away.

'What?' she says again, though she's grinning now.

'A fly is an insect,' I tell her.

She kisses me goodbye, first on the mouth, then on both sides of my nostrils.

'Your nose wings,' she says.

I have brought a book with me, but can't take in any of the words. My father's dead, I keep saying to myself. My father's dead. I glance at my fellow passengers. They're behaving as if it's a day like any other. I put the book back in my bag and take out Dad's last letter, dated 30 January.

I'm still feeling short of breath, which isn't very pleasant, however I must just put up with it. That sentence now seems like a cry for help, and once again I'm surprised at myself for not having reacted. As a rule, Dad would send me a letter every fortnight, and I remember wondering, halfway through February, why he hadn't written. But I let another week go by. Still I didn't ring. I suppose I must have been trying to save money. As I slide the letter back into its envelope, I notice that half my address is missing. Dad wrote the name of the street, but forgot to include the house number, and he omitted the postcode entirely. With hindsight, it's a miracle the letter arrived at all. The inaccuracy of the address and his reference to being short of breath suggest he was in distress. How is it that I didn't realize?

I turn to my window and its expanse of pure blue sky. Far below, the North Sea wrinkles, a ship pinned to the surface like a brooch. *My father's dead.* All of a sudden I feel unbelievably light and free. My body floods with a secret exhilaration. I could be a spy. I could be famous. I could be on my way to meet someone I'm in love with.

Once I have collected my suitcase and my typewriter, I hurry through customs and take an escalator down to the station. My train isn't due for fifteen minutes. I set my luggage down and stroll along the platform. Though clammy, the air smells burnt, metallic, as if some electrical device has shorted out. I gaze across the fields. Recent heavy rain has flattened the stands of bracken in the nearby railway cut, and there's the constant distant sound of water trickling.

England.

Walking back, I notice a tall, burly man staring at me. His mackintosh is beige, like a detective's, its belt fastened tightly, almost chastely, round his midriff, but his hat, a dark brown Homburg with a creamy satin band, looks as if it might belong to a jazz musician. As I approach, he gestures at my suitcase, then says, in an American accent, 'I was beginning to think there was a bomb in there.'

'You can't be too careful these days,' I say.

We look at each other, and even though we're referring to recent terrorist attacks – only two months have passed since Harrods was targeted by the IRA – we both laugh quietly.

The train arrives. Still standing twenty feet apart, we smile and shrug, then enter different carriages. Once I have found a seat, I gaze out of the window at stations whose names I know by heart. Haywards Heath, Three Bridges. Wivelsfield. After my mother died, Dad sent me away to boarding-school, and this was the railway line I would use. I was never in any doubt about what waited for me at the other end – twelve weeks of noise, cold and hunger – and then there were the horrors that couldn't be predicted, or even imagined . . . When I was fourteen, Robin started at the same school, and we would travel together. By then, I no longer dreaded term-time, but Robin would sit across from me, his face so pale that all his freckles showed, his left eye twitching. I would do my best to reassure him. It'll be all right, I'd say. I'll be there, remember? But I wouldn't. Not after lights out, or when the masters weren't around – not when it mattered most. In his first year we would meet on Sundays, after chapel. Our walks would take us beyond the school's ring fence and into the surrounding woods and fields. I was no longer impatient with him, as I had been when we were young. I didn't mind if he dawdled;

there was nowhere we were trying to get to. Sometimes he would tell me what was troubling him, but mostly he kept quiet. It was enough to have the company, a familiar face, an hour or two when he could feel safe. At least, that was how it seemed to me.

From Eastbourne station I take a taxi, and in no time at all we're turning into Summerdown Road. We pull up outside the house. Half hidden by the yew trees in the front garden, it has a withdrawn or injured look, like a person wearing an eye-patch. The wooden fence is badly warped, its grey boards on the point of collapsing outwards on to the pavement, and there are cracks and kinks in the tarmac surface of the drive. The windows are blank; it has been dark for hours, but Robin hasn't thought to draw the curtains. Though my father has just died, what the house reminds me of, as always, is the absence of my mother, and as I step out of the taxi it occurs to me that I might never be able to feel that desolation in its entirety. It's as if my grief is a jigsaw, and I can only deal with one piece at a time.

After paying the driver, I watch as his tail-lights vanish down the hill. I think about my last visit, in November, and how my father locked me out. I remember watching through the letter box as he fumbled his way downstairs. *All the years go by, but you never forget the sound of your child calling you* . . . I could call him now, and there would be no answer. I could keep on calling. He would not appear. He will never hear my voice again. Fingers pick my heart up like a pack of cards and shuffle it. I walk to the front door and put my luggage down, then I reach out for the knocker.

He Didn't Say Goodbye

In 2007 I went to see Bernard, a Frenchman who had been one of Dad's few friends. What could he tell me about my father? He had known him as well as anyone. On a chilly, misty afternoon, I joined the rush-hour traffic streaming out of Eastbourne. Bernard lived outside the town, in Polegate, and I had to negotiate a series of dual carriage-ways and roundabouts, none of which had existed when I was growing up. As I drew closer, I noticed increasing signs of deprivation and neglect. One front garden was buried under a tangle of discarded furniture: a mustard-coloured sofa, a torn mattress, an ironing-board. Nearby, on the pavement, was a naked plastic baby that had lost an arm. A police car passed me in low gear.

I hadn't seen Bernard since the summer of 1984, but when he came to the door, his blurred figure looming behind a panel of frosted glass, he seemed surprisingly familiar. He was immaculate, as always – 'I have just been teaching, you see?' – in a dark suit and tie and a pair of highly polished shoes. He sounded the same too, his voice plummy but slightly nasal, as if he had a history of sinus problems. Only his hair had altered: once black and shiny, it had turned a creamy white, especially on top of his head, where it folded sideways, reminding me of a seagull's wing.

I followed Bernard into the kitchen. While waiting for the kettle to boil, he laid out blueberry muffins and iced slices on a plate. When I remarked, tongue in cheek, on the beauty of the arrangement, he giggled. There had always been a demure, self-effacing quality about Bernard that invited gentle teasing. We carried the tea and cakes into the living-room and sat down at his dining-table.

I started by asking how he met my father.

Determined to avoid military service, he fled to England when he was seventeen, Bernard said, and took a job with Major Tolley, an elderly bachelor and one-time British amateur golf champion. In return for various domestic duties, he was given board and lodging, pocket money, and a free weekly English lesson with my father, who happened to live round the corner. Though Dad was already in his mid-forties by then, the two men immediately got on. 'The sense of humour,' Bernard said, by way of explanation. 'He always liked a good joke.'

I wondered how much Bernard had known about the fragile state of my father's health.

'I vaguely remembered that he'd been wounded. In the navy. Something to do with torpedoes . . .' Bernard began to titter, and this time I found myself joining in.

By the early seventies, Bernard was studying English at a college in town, but he stayed in contact with my father, and when Dad and his new wife, Sonya, had their second child, they asked Bernard if he would be the godfather. Later, when the Home Office lost Bernard's papers, Dad wrote several letters on his behalf, which helped to keep him in the country.

On Tolley's death in 1978, Bernard ran into financial difficulties. Though the major had left him money in a trust, he had no income and nowhere to live. He stayed with the major's gardener for a while, in Polegate. In time, he became a gardener himself. He worked for local families like the Martins and the Goodchilds, and for my father too. In fine weather, he would turn up every week. 'We were always in touch. Yes, indeed.'

I told Bernard how unusual he was, which triggered another fit of the giggles. Unusual, I went on, in that he was one of the only people Dad had thought of as a friend. This revelation seemed to take Bernard aback, and as I began to describe how solitary Dad's life had been, especially towards the end, he interrupted me. 'One thing I do remember,' he said. 'Before your father died, or before he went to the hospital, he rang me up.'

'Did he?'

'He more or less made it clear that this was the end.'

'*Really?*'

'I just said, No, no, it's not true . . .' At the time, Bernard hadn't suspected this would be the last conversation they would ever have, though he had known my father wasn't well.

Had my father told him what was wrong?

'Not really, no.'

A clock chimed somewhere, playing a descending scale.

'He must have known something really final was happening,' Bernard said.

I explained why I was so startled by what he had told me. Dad hadn't phoned any of us, I said, neither before being admitted to hospital, nor while he was there. He had taken his diary with him, which had all our numbers in it, but he hadn't called to let us know where he was. It was only by sheer chance that we had found out. Bernard suggested that perhaps our father hadn't wanted to upset us. That was what I used to think, I said – until just now. Dad was always saying things like that. *I didn't want to upset you.* And it would make sense as a theory if he expected to be discharged in a day or two, but not if he was convinced that he was going to die. 'That's right.' Bernard was staring at the table. 'Yes. Yes, indeed.'

I asked whether Dad had said goodbye to him.

'Well, he didn't say goodbye exactly, but he did say, Oh, I don't think I'll be coming back . . .'

We circled the subject for another twenty minutes, but got no further. Eventually, I thanked Bernard for agreeing to see me, and for the tea, and rose from the table. Outside, the wind gusted and nagged, smelling of chips. As I walked to the kerb, a police car nosed past, and I remembered how, at one point, Bernard had referred to vandalism – though, characteristically, he had used the word 'nuisance'. It seemed a bleak and unforgiving place for somebody so gentle to end up, and filled with affection for him I turned around to offer one last wave, but he had already retreated behind his frosted-glass front door.

Later, I left my hotel on Marine Parade and stood on the damp pavement, looking west. A single string of yellow bulbs looped the entire length of the pier. Fixed to the roof of the main pavilion was the word FUNTASIA, its neon a smudgy, brooding red. I crossed the road. Beyond the railings, banks of shingle sloped steeply down into the dark. A brisk wind was blowing from the south; clouds of vapour that smelled of seaweed and rusting metal lifted past my face. I paused again by a kiosk, its wares described in brash blue capitals: ROCK FUDGE INFLATABLES. The words belonged to another age – naive, comical, but tender too, somehow. I thought of the Channel Bar on the end of the pier, where Robin and I had spent an evening in 1984, and how we had stared in fascination and disbelief as a man who called himself 'Mr Music' played versions of top-ten classics on a Hammond organ. Perhaps I would sit in the bar for an hour. Get a drink, something to eat.

I stepped on to the pier. It had been raining, and the wooden slats were slippery. In the old days, there would be posters advertising shows at the Winter Garden or the Hippodrome. Wrestlers with exaggerated, melancholy names. Pop-stars who hadn't had a hit in years. Comedians. I passed the glass-blowing studio with its shelves of prancing animals, then a domed pavilion crammed with jingle-playing slot-machines. Several notices warned me of the dangers of jumping off the pier. Prosecution, among others. Two teenage boys slouched in a doorway, hoods pulled level with their eyebrows, cigarettes glowing sullenly between their fingers. This was the town I had always longed to leave, for ever.

Halfway along the pier, I looked to the west again. The tide was low. Waves were breaking far out to sea and rushing shorewards in ragged white lines. Their constant, breathy roar erased all other sounds. On the promenade the lit windows of hotel rooms blurred and wobbled in the spray. The phone call Bernard had described was gnawing at me. *I don't think I'll be coming back.* Had my father had some sort of premonition? Or had he simply decided to let go? He had stayed alive for us while we were children, all those years, but now we were gone. We didn't need him any more. Whatever the truth was, I was still surprised that he had failed to summon us. We could so easily have been there, at his bedside.

Turning back into the wind, I walked on towards the

bar. Why had he denied us the opportunity to be with him? Had he become disillusioned with us? Were we a disappointment to him? Had he *deliberately* died alone? This possibility had never occurred to me before, and it brought me to a standstill again, a charred feeling in my throat. His second wife, Sonya, had abandoned him. Perhaps he saw his sons as having abandoned him as well. What had he said to me on my last visit? *We didn't have much time, did we?* If we didn't need him, he didn't need us. He had a stubborn pride in him. There might also have been, as Robin had suggested once, a streak of sarcasm. He would not call. He would not *disturb* us. He would do it on his own, with no support, no charity. Was that what he had thought?

I reached the end of the pier. The bar had a new name – the Atlantis – but its door was padlocked, and no lights were on. I remembered the words on that kiosk. ROCK FUDGE INFLATABLES. Like a series of blows, they now seemed to promise damage, injury. I faced back towards the land. The clammy swirl of the wind, the rushing of those waves.

The season was over.

Chubb

I stand by the front door of the house where I grew up. My life in West Berlin already feels unreal, despite the fact that I was in the city only hours ago. I knock twice, loudly. With Dad gone, there's no need to be quiet any more, not even late at night.

The door opens. Before I can speak, Robin leans close to me and whispers, 'Ralph and Vivian are here.'

I stare at him. Ralph, my brother, and Vivian, his wife.

'They arrived this morning,' Robin says in the same dramatic whisper. 'They're moving in.'

'I thought Ralph worked in London.'

'He does. He's going to try and change his job.'

I glance sideways, into the dark. All day, I have been imagining that Robin and I would have the house to ourselves. Once the funeral was over, we would stay up until dawn, drinking and talking, listening to music. At weekends, there would be parties, with people driving down from London. It would be a last wild farewell to the place where everything began. If Ralph and Vivian are living with us, though, there will be constraints.

Not that Robin seems too bothered. 'You'd better come in.' As I step over the threshold, he grins at me across one shoulder. 'We've been opening Dad's wine.'

I follow him into the kitchen. Ralph is sitting where Dad used to sit, in the blue wooden chair at the head of the table. Vivian is at right angles to him, her back to the door. She only half-turns when I walk in. Her dark hair falls well past her shoulders, the same length as it was three years ago. I seem to recognize her sweater too, the knitted wool flecked with grey, white and pale blue. The air in the room is tense, smoky.

Bending, I kiss Vivian, then turn to Ralph. He rises to his feet, and his face crumples into a smile that manages to be wry, affectionate and bashful, all at the same time. Something about the shape of his top lip reminds me that he used to play the trumpet. I wonder if he still does. We hug each other quickly. It occurs to me that, since I'm the last to arrive, Ralph and Vivian will have been waiting for me, and not, I imagine, without some apprehension. We have become riddles to one another. Unknown quantities.

I take off my black oilskin and drape it across the chair behind the door, then I pour myself a glass of wine from the open bottle and sit down at the far end of the table. I lean back, light a cigarette. Ralph glances at Robin, and I know what he's thinking. *He still smokes.* I tell them that what has happened hasn't really sunk in yet. It all just seems so unbelievable. There are nods. Ralph and Vivian reach for their own cigarettes. The atmosphere loosens a notch.

And suddenly all four of us are smoking, even though no one has ever lit up in the kitchen before – nor, for that matter, in the house. Dad attributed his lung problems to cigarettes, and when we were boys he would often lecture us on how dangerous they were. To be smoking now feels disrespectful, even risky, and my eyes keep flicking towards the door, afraid he might appear at any moment. From time to time Vivian goes upstairs to check on Greta, who is six months old. Ralph and Vivian have a baby. That, too, seems unbelievable.

I talk about the self-important feeling I had while on the plane. Almost as if I were a celebrity. I shrug. But my brothers are nodding again. They felt something similar. Our lives seem to have been heightened or even somehow *invigorated* by our father's death. Is this normal? Every now and then, a silence falls. Difficult tasks lie ahead of us. We will have to choose a funeral director. We will need to contact Dad's relatives and friends. And there will be a visit to the hospital – a chance to see Dad for the last time.

Robin leaves the room to fetch more wine. 'At least we won't have to buy anything to drink for a while,' he says when he returns. 'There must be twenty bottles in the study.'

'He always saved his wine for special occasions.' My voice is momentarily unsteady.

'This *is* a special occasion,' Ralph says.

Vivian has hardly opened her mouth all evening. She keeps her eyes on Ralph, and if she does speak, she speaks to Ralph, even though she might be responding to me or Robin. When you try and point something out to a cat, it tends to stare at the end of your finger. That's what talking to Vivian is like.

I ask where everyone is sleeping. Ralph says he has taken 'Paradise', so called because it has a dressing-room whose window looks towards Paradise Wood; the word has been on the door for as long as I can remember, the light-blue letters painted at head-height on the dark brown varnish. Robin tells me he is using Dad's room. Unwilling to start searching for clean sheets, I decide to share Dad's double bed with Robin.

I climb the stairs. On reaching the landing, I take a breath, then open Dad's door. Nothing has changed. In front of me is the fireplace that he boarded up with one of his own paintings to stop the draughts, and on the chimney breast above is his only valuable possession – a framed lithograph by Georges Braque. To my right are the curtains he bought with Sonya in the early seventies, columns of white shapes that resemble snowflakes overlapping dizzily on a background of cobalt and turquoise. In the far corner, above the sink, is his green glass bottle of eucalyptus oil. On nights when I agreed to massage his back, he would stand the bottle in warm water so it heated up to body temperature.

I slip between the sheets. The bed still smells of him – lavender soap and talcum powder – but I can smell cigarette smoke too. Old rules are being broken, thirty years collapsing in an instant. I wonder if I should say something, now that I am head of the family. What would Dad expect of me? The impossible, I suppose – as always. I have so obviously failed to live up to his ideals. I should have claimed that Scottish title. I should have married a girl from a good family. He wanted me to be a professional golfer as well. So many should haves. But I'm too tired to think, or care. My head sinks on to the pillow, and I'm gone.

I wake to the sound of hammering. Forcing my eyes open, I imagine for a few moments that I'm in Kreuzberg, but there is no shadow on the ceiling, no black paint lurking underneath the white. These dark blue sheets, this dark blue pillow: I'm lying in my father's bed. I turn my head. Robin is fast asleep beside me. Two parallel lines run diagonally towards his left eyebrow, as though a small but heavy vehicle drove across his forehead in the night. Beyond him, on a chair, is a jug of water. If he drinks the contents of the jug before he goes to sleep, he doesn't get a hangover. So he claims. The hammering becomes a little more insistent.

I sit up. 'Rob?'

'What?' he murmurs, eyes still closed.

'That noise.'

'Fuck. What is it?'

'I don't know.'

The banging stops, then starts again, even louder than before.

'Sounds like it's coming from inside the house,' I say.

I ease out of bed and pull on trousers and a shirt. Robin groans and hauls himself upright. Opening Dad's door, I step out on to the landing. With Robin at my shoulder, I peer round the corner. Outside Paradise is a dusty-looking man in paint-stained overalls. He appears to be attacking a point about halfway up the door, close to the handle.

I say hello.

The man glances round in a casual, almost insolent manner. He doesn't seem to realize that he has woken us up – or, if he does, he isn't overly concerned. Set into the door behind him is a lock the size of a fist, its bright brass standing out against the ancient varnish.

'This is a good lock, this is,' he says, his bottom lip jutting briefly. 'This is a Chubb. Best lock there is.' He nods, lending weight to his judgement, then turns back to the door. The hammering continues.

Robin and I retreat to Dad's room. I lean against the windowsill, arms folded. Robin sits on the edge of the bed and rubs his eyes.

'That's a good lock, that is,' he says after a while.

'It's a Chubb,' I say.

'You don't get better than a Chubb.'

We chuckle quietly.

'It seems a bit extreme,' I say, 'don't you think?'

'Maybe they're frightened.'

'What of?'

Robin shrugs. 'Us, I suppose.'

I remember a weekend in 1978. I had arrived in East-bourne with a lump of hash zipped into my leather jacket, and on the Saturday night Robin and I got stoned in his bedroom, which was downstairs, at the front of the house. Instead of rolling joints, we used a technique that involved a jam jar, a needle and half a cork. That way, if Dad walked in, there would be nothing for him to smell. We opened the window as well, though, just to be on the safe side. As we sat in Robin's room, rain tapping softly on the leaves of the holly bush outside, we wondered what would become of Dad now that Sonya had left him. He was disabled. He had little or no money. He was almost sixty.

'Maybe we should do away with him,' I said.

I tilted the jar for Robin, who put his mouth to the gap and sucked out all the smoke. Fixed on the end of the needle, the hash continued to burn – a tiny, glowing coal.

'You know,' I said, 'put him out of his misery.'

When Robin finally exhaled, I looked at him and we both began to shake with laughter. Soon we were laughing so hard we could scarcely breathe.

'How,' Robin gasped, 'are we going to do it?'

As we ran through the various methods, we rolled on the floor in absolute hysterics.

'Stop.' Robin was clutching his ribs. 'It hurts.'

'I can't,' I said. I couldn't work out what was so funny, but that only made it worse.

Later, when there was no more smoke in the jar, we drifted, each in his own reverie. I saw my father lying in the doorway in his dressing-gown, his face turned towards me, his eyes wide open. Offshore, a foghorn sounded. The rain had stopped, and the air seemed polished, crystalline. The hush of a seaside resort in winter.

Towards midnight, we climbed out of the window and on to the drive. The clouds had broken up; sky showed in the gaps like black glass. We stood on the street corner, shoulders hoisted, sharing a cigarette. Drips fell from the trees.

'Do you think we woke him up?' Robin said.

'I hope not,' I said. 'I mean, imagine if he'd heard . . .'

The hammering is still going on.

Standing at Dad's bedroom window, I wonder if Ralph knows about that night in 1978. I don't think I ever told him, but Robin might have done.

Ralph and Vivian met in 1979, during their first term at London University. Vivian had grown up in an industrial city in the West Midlands. With her black eyeliner and her long dark hair, I used to think she looked like Chrissie Hynde, the lead singer of the Pretenders. Vivian and my brother quickly became inseparable. They went to each other's lectures. They ate together. They rarely, if ever, spent a night apart.

When I first knew them as a couple, they were renting a

bedsit in Princes Square, not far from Hyde Park. That year I was living with my girlfriend Tina in a council flat south of the river. Both Ralph and I had motorbikes, and Tina and Vivian rode pillion. The four of us would go to pubs or live music venues – the Nashville Rooms, the Moonlight Club. But then, almost overnight, Ralph and Vivian stopped calling, and the next time they moved they didn't give us their address.

In the autumn of 1980, while returning from a job interview, I found myself in Bayswater. I rode to the house where they had lived and parked outside. As I loitered on the pavement, the front door opened and a West Indian appeared, eyes narrowed against the morning light, cigarette smoke coiling like a blue vine up his arm. Could this be the famous Pedro, who had once chased Vivian round the basement kitchen with a knife? As he started down the steps, I eased past him, catching the door before it clicked shut. I climbed the stairs to the first floor and paused outside the room that Ralph and Vivian used to rent. It was so quiet on the landing that I could hear a fly rebounding off the windowpane behind me. I thought about my last visit, and how I had sat on the floor and watched as Vivian dyed Ralph's hair. The room had been stuffy and cramped, with yellow walls, and they had told me about the people in the building – a Glaswegian on parole, a Jesus look-alike, a pimp. I reached out and knocked on the door. I wasn't sure what I would say if somebody answered. *Hello. I'm looking for my brother.* Upstairs, a kettle came to the boil. Its whistling built to a crescendo, then cut out. I felt close to Ralph, even though I knew he was no longer there. I was standing where he would have stood if he was fitting his key into the lock. I was breathing the same air.

Back at our flat in the Oval, Tina and I kept trying to

work out what lay behind Ralph's abrupt disappearance. Tina had met Ralph while at art college in Eastbourne – being a friend of Robin's, she had often run into Ralph at parties or in pubs – and she would constantly circle back to the idea that she was to blame. She felt she might have been indiscreet about Ralph's past, and that Vivian might have taken offence, but I could never grasp the nature of the indiscretion. So far as I knew, Vivian had been Ralph's first real girlfriend, his first – and only – true love.

A few months later, on the phone, Dad told me that Ralph and Vivian were always moving from one flat to another, and that he couldn't keep up with the changes of address.

'Why is that, do you think?' I asked.

He couldn't say.

In that same phone call, he told me he would hear them walking around the house in the middle of the night. He had no idea how they got in. He thought they were taking things.

'How could you be sure it was them?'

'I heard the motorbike.'

He wanted to ask them what they were doing, but was afraid to leave his room. By morning, he said, they would usually be gone.

I didn't know what to make of this. Why would my brother and his girlfriend bother to ride all the way from London to Eastbourne, a distance of more than seventy miles? And even if they did, what would they take from the house? Perhaps Dad had been dreaming – or perhaps he was becoming confused. Perhaps this was what happened when you took barbiturates night after night, year after year . . .

It must have been at around this time that Robin

showed me a photo of Ralph standing on the drive. Ralph was dressed in a black leather jacket and narrow black trousers. His feet were encased in heavy-duty motorcycle boots. His hair, liquorice-black, stuck up in a towering Mohican, and his mouth twisted in a trademark Billy Idol sneer. Wraparound sunglasses hid his eyes. Outlined against the eggshell-blue of the garage doors, he looked as though he had just teleported in from some post-apoca-lyptic future. I thought the picture was wonderful, but I could understand why Dad might be dismayed or even threatened by his son's new incarnation. It was Dad's belief that Ralph had undergone a profound change since meet-ing Vivian, not only in appearance, but psychologically. He was convinced that Ralph had fallen under her spell, and he had taken to calling her 'Svengali' – though not, I imag-ined, to her face. In an underhand and vicious poem – one of the most impassioned that he ever wrote – he portrayed her slouching on a chair in the kitchen, picking her nose. With her 'racoon eyes' fixed on Dad, she whispered poi-sonous instructions into Ralph's ear. It occurred to me that Dad feared physical assault.

When I put all these fragments together, I couldn't help but see Ralph and Vivian as a kind of latter-day Bonnie and Clyde, yet they hadn't committed any crimes, and nobody was after them – at least, not so far as I knew. Though maybe the truth was subtler than that. Suppose Ralph and Vivian *themselves* felt under threat? What if they saw the world as malicious, parasitical, destructive? They had found each other, and they weren't about to let anything – or any*one* – come between them. There was a sense in which the feral nature of their intimacy was romantic – the spurning of the world, the wariness, the constant flight – but didn't it also smack of paranoia?

The silence was finally broken in the spring of 1981 by the arrival of a letter. Ralph had written to tell me that he and Vivian were planning to get married and to ask if I would be his best man. Not having seen him or even spoken to him for more than a year, I felt as though a chasm had opened up between us. I had heard that he had become a Catholic – he had spent time in a monastery, apparently, undergoing rites of Christian initiation; Vivian's family were calling him 'the Convert' – and while this story had the ring of authenticity, Vivian herself being a Catholic, I'd had no choice but to file it away with all the other stories I'd been told. To me, Ralph was not unlike the Scarlet Pimpernel – a figure shrouded in rumour and hearsay, none of it verifiable. I wrote back saying that he should find somebody else. I tried to explain my thinking. A best man ought to be a person who was close to the groom, I said – a confidant, in other words – and since we had fallen out of touch I viewed myself as being unequal to the role, if not actually inadequate.

When the wedding day came, Robin travelled up from Newport, where he was now at art college. Though Tina and I were still living together, her name had been omitted from my invitation, which seemed to confirm her theory that she was to blame for the rift. Robin and I caught a bus to Hampstead. Robin wore a green tweed suit he had bought from a charity shop in Wales. My suit was also green. Borrowed from Dad, it had been hanging in his bedroom cupboard since the late sixties, and smelled acridly of mothballs and dust. My hair was dyed Natural Red, as usual. According to the instructions on the packet, you were supposed to wash the henna out after twenty minutes, but I always left it for about three hours, just to make quite sure it worked. Robin's hair was a curious whitish-yellow. He had bleached it himself, using hydrogen peroxide. Only the week before, he had met Dennis Potter, the famous TV dramatist and playwright, who told him that he looked like a badly upholstered settee.

Arriving at the church, Robin and I loitered on the edge of a crowd of people we didn't recognize. These, presumably, were Vivian's family and friends. Naively, perhaps, we were unprepared for the reception we received, which veered from coldness and suspicion to outright hostility. While we were waiting to go in, a man in a dark blue suit with a flamboyant chalk pinstripe strolled aggressively towards us, his chin lifted, as though daring one of us to land a blow. He wanted to know why we were against the marriage.

'We're not against the marriage,' I said. 'Why would we be here . . .' My voice petered out.

Hands in his pockets, the man looked at me for a long moment, one corner of his mouth curling, then he turned on his heel and walked away.

Vivian's relatives were convinced of our antagonism, and our family's meagre turnout did nothing to dislodge that belief. Dad had stayed at home – though that, in itself, didn't mean much. Even if he had approved of the wedding, he wouldn't have gone; he didn't go to anything. My mother's brother, Frank, and his wife, Miriam, hadn't appeared either. In Cornwall that week, they had been unwilling to interrupt their holiday. There was no sign of my stepmother, Sonya, and her two children, Rosie and Halliday, but then Ralph might not have invited them. Was my father's brother, Roland, there? Possibly. My cousins? I'm not sure. I seem to remember a number of Vivian's relations having to be shifted on to our side of the church so as to make things look less embarrassing.

Seeing Ralph at the altar, I was surprised at the change in him. Gone was all trace of the swaggering Mohican, gone the Billy Idol sneer. His hair was cropped, and he looked pallid and gaunt, like somebody who had been fasting. I remembered the golden quality he'd had about him at fifteen, an almost carnal glow, and wondered what he had been through. Had Dad been right to worry?

'Was he always that pale?' I whisper in Robin's ear.

'He doesn't look very happy, does he?'

'Perhaps he's nervous . . .'

We may not have been against the marriage, Robin and I, but at the same time neither of us took the idea very seriously. To us, it seemed at once bizarre and conventional, a bit of a joke.

We have so much to arrange during the days leading up to the funeral that we struggle to keep up. Functioning in a group seems to help. As I write to Hanne, *We all go round together, in a little army.* No one has mentioned the man in the paint-stained overalls or the loud hammering, but the episode seems to hover in the air between us if we're all in the same room, and once, when the word 'lock' crops up in a sentence, Robin slides a glance my way, one eyebrow cocked. I feel Ralph and Vivian have called our bluff. They acted without asking our permission, and we haven't dared even to raise the subject, let alone protest. What we're left with is an uneasy spirit of accommodation – the idea that the boat must not, under any circumstances, be rocked. Is this cowardice or common sense? I can't decide. The whole set-up's unusual. I've never heard of anybody doing what we're doing. A father dies. His three sons return to the family home, start living there . . . Sometimes I have the feeling we're made up – characters in a story, part of a myth. We're like children again, but with no parents. We're on our own, and completely in the dark.

I'm tempted to take Ralph aside and tell him there's no need for such radical measures, but either Vivian appears as I'm about to speak or else I hesitate too long and the moment is lost. Maybe, in the end, I feel I'm on shaky ground. What do I know about their needs? I have no idea what is going on in Ralph's head – to say nothing of Vivian's. Clearly, they trust no one, least of all those closest to them, and they are more determined than ever to safeguard what is theirs, especially now they have a child.

But a lock, though?

Do they still believe that we're against them? Do they honestly think we wish them harm? If so, why move back into the house? Why take that risk?

I walk downstairs one morning to find the kitchen door ajar. A mysterious, repetitive grating or scraping sound is coming from inside the room. Vivian has her back to the door, as usual, and she is bent over the table, her right elbow working rhythmically. Greta is sitting in a high chair beyond her.

Pushing the door open, I say good morning. Greta bangs the tray in front of her with a plastic beaker. I step closer, then peer over Vivian's shoulder. In her left hand is Dad's grindstone, concave on both sides from years of use, but the knife she's sharpening isn't one I recognize.

She speaks before I can frame a question.

'It's a flick knife,' she says. 'Ralph's got one too.' She leans back and tests the blade against her thumb.

'What for?' I say.

'So we can defend ourselves.'

I nod slowly.

'They're identical,' she says.

Later, as I replay the encounter, I have the sneaking suspicion that she was hoping either Robin or I would catch her sharpening that knife. It was a gesture of defiance, a show of strength. She wanted us to know that she and Ralph are not to be taken lightly. First the Chubb lock, now the flick knives.

So we can defend ourselves.

That evening, in the sitting-room, I tell Ralph that I saw Vivian's knife, and that she said he carries one as well. Without a word, he reaches into his jacket pocket and produces a knife that is an exact replica of hers. When I ask him how it works, he presses a small button on the handle, and a long thin blade springs out. Eyes lowered, face consumed with a sort of quiet, almost mystical relish, he balances the knife on the palm of his hand. The steel reflects a neat slice of the ceiling. Does he take the knife to work with him? Is he prepared to use it?

'Jesus, Ralph,' I say, 'you're dangerous.'

His eyes lift from the blade.

He smiles.

Call Me by My Proper Name

My mother's brother was christened Cedric, but people always called him Joe. As a child, I don't remember seeing Uncle Joe, not even once. All kinds of stories were told about him, though. A brilliant scholar, of whom great things were expected, he was expelled from public school for taking a group of younger boys to the cinema in Maidstone. In his early twenties, he was offered a job by the London Bank of South America. He flew to Colombia. Within a few months of landing in Bogotá, he moved out of the approved lodgings for single employees and registered in a hotel under an assumed identity. He had sex with local women. He grew a beard. The bank transferred him to a less prestigious branch in Ecuador. A year later, in circumstances that have never been entirely clear to me, Joe was deported. Back in England, he joined the army, but since his superiors at the bank had given him a one-line reference, stating merely that he had been in their employ, he wasn't considered officer material. Sent out to Korea, he managed to avoid active duty. He also managed to burn down a hut belonging to the regiment. On returning from the war, he worked down a coal mine, then in a petrol station on the A5. Later, he delivered milk. In his mid-forties, he took to his bed, sleeping naked in sheets that were soaked in olive oil. He claimed it was good for his skin. The beard grew again, longer this time. He lived on boiled rice and packets of Benson & Hedges. If family members tried to visit, he would tell them to bugger off. Most years, a Christmas card would arrive at our house, signed 'Uncle Joe', or he would send a mouldy bar of chocolate, which would immediately be consigned to the dustbin, but Joe himself remained an enigma. The few facts I was able to gather only made him harder to imagine; he seemed to disappear behind them, as one might disappear behind a wig and a false nose. All Dad would ever say was that he was a 'bad influence', and that Wendy, our mother, had been frightened of him, and had avoided him; Dad seemed to worry that we, his sons, might have inherited Joe's genes, and might end up the same way. In the late seventies, Joe's life took yet another turn, perhaps the most unlikely one of all: he became a Muslim. Suddenly he wasn't Cedric any more, or even Uncle Joe. He was Abdul Rauf.

In 1986, Joe's brother, Frank, offered to take me to see him. By then Joe was living in Wolverhampton, in a place called Penndale Lodge, which Frank gave me to understand was some sort of refuge for destitute old men. From Four Oaks, the private estate where Frank and Miriam lived, it was a forty-minute drive, and within a quarter of an hour of setting out the landscape began to deteriorate. During the nineteenth century, Wolverhampton had been a thriving industrial centre, with a huge steel works, several well-established coach-builders, and a famous bicycle manufacturer – great fortunes had been made in the town – but now, on every side, there were boarded-up shops, derelict factories, and vacant lots littered with builders' rubble and broken glass.

As we drove through this urban wasteland, I turned to Frank. 'I hadn't realized how run-down it was round here.'

'Oh, it's terrible,' he said, 'just *terrible*.'

He stopped in a suburb called Whitmore Reans, outside a scruffy grocery store whose sign was in Arabic. When he returned, he was clutching two brown-paper bags. He told me he had bought some things he thought Joe might appreciate.

After driving for a few more minutes, we turned into a narrow street of terraced housing. Penndale Lodge – the name was on the gatepost – had a dull red-brick façade and grubby windows, and its front door was painted a shade of blue that reminded me of the police. My stomach tightened, and in an attempt to quieten my nerves I started talking. 'It doesn't look much like a lodge to me.'

'I know.' Frank's eyebrows lifted until they were almost at right angles to each other, and his eyes squeezed shut. 'He just dragged himself down, Joe did. He was *determined* to drag himself down. All the way to the gutter.'

'You told me a story once,' I said, 'about the time he showed up on your doorstep. He'd been living rough, in Birmingham . . .'

'Did I?'

'He hadn't changed his clothes for weeks, apparently. He smelled awful.' Miriam had told me that Joe had been wearing his underpants for so long that it was impossible to work out what colour they had been when they were new.

'Yes.' Frank was nodding now, but with the same anguished expression. 'Yes, yes, I think that's right.'

My probing always seemed to put Frank under pressure. I was after details that would bring Joe to life, but these were the very details Frank concealed from himself. I imagined Joe must have been truly desperate to have thrown himself on his brother's mercy; in the stories I had heard, he came across as a proud man, somebody who would go to almost any lengths to avoid invoking pity or condescension. I recalled another snippet of information Frank had once let slip.

'He was diagnosed as a schizophrenic, wasn't he?'

'I think so,' Frank said wearily. 'I'm not sure. He was in the same hospital as Mummy for a while – St Andrews, in Northampton.'

'When was that?'

'In the fifties. Fifty-seven or eight. I was in there too.'

I turned and looked at him. 'Were you? What for?'

'I had a breakdown. It was worrying about the mill that did it. Waiting to take over the mill, and Eric being such a bastard about it all.'

Eric was Frank's uncle – my great-uncle – and the mill was a family business that Eric used to own and run. Built of smoke-blackened brick, and dating from the early Victorian period, it had a flat roof, tottering chimneys, and row upon row of tall, blind windows, and it stood beside a sleepy, desolate canal whose water was permanently hidden by a skin of pale green algae. It took ninety women to operate the weaving machines, and I had always been intrigued by what they manufactured: the tape and webbing could be transformed into the loops in the back of a pair of boots, the edging of a horse blanket, or the straps on a rucksack or a parachute. As retirement approached, Eric had needed to start thinking about a successor. Since he had never married or had children, his eldest nephew, Frank, was the obvious choice, but Eric had constantly threatened to overlook him in favour of Norman, an epileptic he already employed in a minor managerial role. He would tell Frank how impressed he was with Norman, how Norman had what it took. Frank, he said, was 'nesh' – local slang for 'incompetent' or 'weak'. It seemed to amuse Eric to play the two men off against each other.

'*God*, he was a bastard,' Frank said.

I had to smile, partly at Frank's language, but also at the way in which he had succeeded in making himself the subject of the conversation. You could ask Frank any question, and it would invariably lead to one of a handful of riffs and rants that now defined his life for him. Still, he had told me something I didn't know: in the late fifties, not long after I was born, my grandmother and two of my uncles were all inmates of the same mental home – and then there was my mother, Wendy, with her so-called 'high spirits' . . . Dad must have wondered what sort of family he had married into.

With a heavy sigh, Frank levered himself out of the car. I followed him through the gate and up to the front door, then watched as he jabbed at the bell with his finger. The woman who answered the door was bulky around the middle, as if she had a pillow strapped on underneath her clothes.

'We've come to see Joe Gausden.' Frank spoke fatalistically, like somebody expecting to be turned away.

The woman stood back and signalled towards a door on the left side of the hall. 'He's in there.'

Frank led me into the front room.

'This is your nephew, Rupert,' he announced.

On the far side of the room, next to a modest fireplace,

sat a man in an ankle-length cream-coloured djellaba and a pale yellow *kufi* skullcap. He had an olive complexion and dark eyes, and both hands were clasped on a cane that stood upright between his sandalled feet. A greying beard reached down over his chest. He was fifty-eight, but looked a decade older. The word 'ayatollah' floated into my mind.

'This is Rupert,' Frank said. 'Wendy's son.'

I crossed to where Joe was sitting. He made no attempt to get to his feet. Instead, he held out his right hand, which I took in mine. Up close, his eyes had a sombre, penetrating quality; I could see no humour there. The two brothers didn't touch, I noticed, or even greet each other.

Now I was over by the fireplace I saw that Joe was not alone in the room. Against the opposite wall were four or five other men, all seated on ramshackle chairs. The way in which they were arranged, in a loose semicircle, and at some distance from Joe, suggested not just that the residents of Penndale Lodge had divided into two camps, but that Joe was viewed as a performer, as entertainment.

I said hello, then took a seat facing my uncle. Frank sat to my right, with his back to the other men. I could see them beyond him, eyeing us with a kind of patient cunning.

Frank held out the two brown-paper bags. 'I bought a few things for you, Joe. I thought you might like them.'

Joe thrust his cane aside, then roughly took the bags. He opened one and peered inside. 'Are they halal?'

Frank's face assumed a look of agony. 'I don't know, Joe. No, I don't think –'

'Then what did you bring them for, you stupid bugger? They're no bloody use to me.' Joe almost slung the paper bags at Frank.

'Halal,' one of the men muttered, and winked at me.

In a voice that had lifted half an octave, Frank was defending himself. He hadn't noticed, he was saying. He didn't *know*. How was he *supposed* to know? He'd driven all the way from Four Oaks, just so Joe could meet his nephew. He'd seen an Islamic shop and bought some things he thought –

Joe didn't appear to be listening. I had the impression he had heard it all before and found it utterly contemptible. Sometimes his eyes would drift towards the bay window, but he seemed indifferent to the world outside. Sometimes, too, he glanced at me, but with such impassivity that I was rendered speechless, almost inanimate. In the end, he fixed his gaze on Frank again. Though he wasn't paying the slightest attention to what Frank was saying, he clearly derived a certain vengeful pleasure from watching his older brother squirm.

'If that's all you're capable of,' he said at last, 'you shouldn't bother coming. If that's all the *respect* you can show.'

'Oh, don't be like that, Joe . . .'

Later, he decided to concentrate on me. He said he could see a family resemblance. There was something of Wendy, he thought. I told him people usually said I looked more like my father. He shrugged. Either he didn't remember my father, or else he just wasn't interested. To my right, I was aware of the old men shifting on their chairs. They sucked their teeth, dropped ash on their cardigans.

'Apparently, Wendy was frightened of you,' I said.

'Who told you that?'

'It must have been my dad.'

Joe's eyes gleamed, and I felt my words had pleased him. He wasn't about to speculate on why somebody might find him frightening. What other people thought was their own affair; it had nothing to do with him. But I was struck by the fact that he seemed flattered by what I'd said. He was a vain man, even if his vanity took a decidedly unusual form. Despite that, I found I wanted him to like me.

'You haven't offered your guests any tea, Cedric,' one of the men said.

My uncle's head lifted sharply, and he glared across the room. 'My name's not Cedric.'

'Come on, Cedric,' another man said, nudging his neighbour. 'You don't have to be like that.'

'Call me by my proper name,' Joe thundered, 'or keep your stupid mouths shut.'

'That *is* your proper name,' the first man said.

'My *name* is Abdul Rauf. How many times do I have to tell you?'

The old men exchanged glances. One was smirking. Another choked on his tea.

Joe raised an arm and pointed across the room at them. 'You're going to bloody burn in hell, the lot of you,' he shouted. 'You're all damned.'

'That's not very nice – '

'That's rude, that is – '

'No need to lose your rag, Ced – '

'You ignorant fucking half-wits. You're all going to burn, you hear me?' Joe's voice was shaking with rage.

I looked at Frank. His head was tilted back, and he had closed his eyes. Of all the people in the room, he seemed to be suffering the most.

During the hour I spent in Penndale Lodge, Joe had two such outbursts, both provoked by personal affronts. The old men were going to burn in hell, not because they were

Christians, or godless, but because they refused to take Joe seriously. Their sin was mockery – a lack of deference. Somehow, though, I felt that Joe had brought this on himself. People didn't see him as a Muslim. He was just somebody who had taken dressing-up a bit too far. He had turned himself into a spectacle – a freak; he had invited ridicule. I thought I understood why Ralph had become a Catholic, but I still couldn't make sense of Joe's conversion to Islam. Was it a matter of genuine faith, or was it an intellectual decision, born out of his lifelong interest in comparative religion? Had he simply adopted a set of values and beliefs that would allow him to rail against a world into which he didn't seem to fit? Or could it have been a calculated attempt to upset the family, to 'stick two fingers up to the lot of us', as Frank had put it once?

I no longer recall what Joe and I said to each other after that. I only remember his physical appearance – the large, expressive hands with their prominent knuckles and blue-black veins; the beard, which was of biblical proportions, reaching almost to his lap; and his eyes, such a dark shade of brown that the pupils and irises were hard to tell apart. I said goodbye, knowing I might never see him again. Had I asked the right questions? Probably not. It had been difficult with all those old men listening – but perhaps it would have been difficult anyway. Joe wasn't exactly forthcoming; one would have had to pick him, like a particularly stubborn lock.

What saddened me as I walked to the car was the thought that he would go on sitting in that front room, day after day, the other residents ranged against him like a Greek chorus, or a jury, or a crowd of hecklers at a comedy club. Intentionally or not, he had contrived a kind of purgatory for himself.

Driving back to Four Oaks, Frank returned to his theme, and it echoed some of what I had been thinking.

'He wouldn't play the game, you see – just *wouldn't play the game*. He was *buggered* if he was going to do what other people wanted. He thought he was above all that. But he wasn't. He wasn't above it.'

I remembered Frank telling me how Joe behaved on the football pitch at school. Joe would have been eight or nine at the time. When the ball bounced towards him, he folded his arms and watched it roll past. Everyone on the touchline was shouting. *Come on, Gausden. Kick it.* But he wouldn't. A goal was scored as a result. The game was lost. He wouldn't even take part, let alone compete.

'He always had to do things his own way,' Frank said, 'and look what happened.'

'He's pretty hard on you,' I said.

'All I ever did was try and help him get back on his feet. The number of times I did that! *God!*'

'Maybe he didn't want to be helped. Maybe you should have left him alone.'

'He was still part of the family . . .'

Frank had missed the point. I was wondering how Joe would have reacted if Frank had called his bluff. *You want to have nothing to do with us? You want us to leave you alone? All right. We will.* But it was too late now.

Back on the dual carriageway, Frank switched lanes without signalling, and the driver of the car behind us had to swerve. He gave us a loud blast on his horn.

'*Now* what?' Frank said.

Death Pyjamas

I unlock my father's bright red Renault and climb behind the steering wheel, then twist the key in the ignition. Exhaust fumes cloud the garage doorway. Two hours' drive away, in Midhurst, his body has been laid out in a chapel of rest.

I follow the coast road, through drowsy, crumbling towns like Peacehaven and Rottingdean. Ralph and Vivian sit in the back with Greta, holding hands. Beside me, in the front, Robin stares straight ahead. His eyes look oddly static in their sockets, and his lips move, one against the other, as though he is trying to moisten them. He only decided to join us at the last minute, saying he didn't like the idea of staying in the house by himself.

We pass all the old landmarks: Saltdean Lido with its blistered white paint and sweeping concrete parapets; the fudge-coloured façade of St Dunstan's Home for the Blind; Brighton's elegant but derelict West Pier. As we turn inland, I wonder whether Robin's sudden change of heart might help to explain how it is that we three brothers have come to be living together in the same house. It's not so much that we didn't trust each other with the funeral arrangements or the execution of the will. It might simply be that none of us wanted to feel left out.

To the north of Midhurst, the road climbs steadily for about a mile, and as I shift down into third I glance into the pines that mass on the left side of the car, their trunks showing through the mist like rusty nails lodged in wax. In my teens, I often kept Dad company when he drove to the hospital for his six-monthly check-ups. Before reporting to his doctor, we would stop at a pub called the Angel for half a pint of bitter and a ploughman's. As Dad told one terrible joke after another, his smile would seem to take up too much room in his face. I don't think I ever realized how nervous he was. On those occasions, he would always have to prepare himself for the worst. They might not allow him to go home. They might have to operate. They might give him only weeks to live. While he was in the hospital, undergoing tests, I would wander through the grounds. I would think of my mother, who had worked in the hospital as a nurse. It was here that my parents had first met. It was here that they had fallen in love. They would have strolled across these lush, striped lawns, beneath these lofty trees. Wendy was dark-haired, voluptuous. Twenty-one. Rod was nine years older. Though the war had destroyed his youth, it had also, paradoxically, kept him young, shielding him from the pressures of an ordinary existence. His black hair was thinning on top, but his face had a beauty that was classical: a strong straight nose, a sculpted mouth. Their first kiss, I was sure, would have taken place in this hushed half-darkness, buttresses of sunlight slanting through the gaps between branches, pine needles scattered, glowing, on the forest floor. The early fifties. The war was over, but only just. Rod had forfeited so much – his fitness, his health, his dreams. As for Wendy, she had lost both parents. Her father had suffered a fatal heart attack when she was seventeen. Within a year, her mother found she couldn't cope and committed herself to an asylum in Northampton. Though still young, Rod and Wendy had been through difficult times, both of them. But now they had each other. Together, they could make a go of it. After what had happened, they had every right to expect life to start working in their favour.

And for a while it did.

A big 'H' appears up ahead, and our faces stiffen. Even the baby has gone quiet. I signal left and turn into the drive. When the hospital finally reveals itself, it looks exclusive. With its white flagpole and its ivy-clad brick walls, it could almost be a country house hotel.

As we wait in reception, I go over my recent phone call with Ilaine, my godmother. Ilaine is a Sufi, and when I told her that I had bad news she took issue with the words. Given the many hardships my father had faced, she believed he had done well to lead such a full life. Look at what was taken from him, she said, and what he did with what remained. However she also felt he had very little left to look forward to, and that this might have been a good time for him to go. She offered me her thoughts on grief. As a Sufi, she saw mourning as a form of selfishness, since mourners are generally only thinking of themselves. All tears do is bind the dead to the earth. People who have died need to rise up, she said, and we shouldn't try and stop them. Since talking to Ilaine, I have begun to incorporate some of her philosophy into the way I handle the other calls I've had to make, and the conversations have become less tortured and more natural.

At last, a sister arrives. She apologizes for the delay; there was an emergency, she says. She leads us down a long passage with a highly polished floor, through doors that swing outwards, then thump back into place behind us. She tells us that our father was well known in the hospital, and very well liked. This carries the faint sting of a rebuke, as though, having noted our dyed hair, our jumble-sale clothing, and our unlikely baby, she has decided that we don't deserve him. One final set of doors, and we're outside. The air is watery and grey, the colour of an empty milk bottle. Crows creak and scuffle in the treetops. We follow the sister along a path that cuts diagonally across an area of grass. My eyelids feel swollen, as if I've just woken up. My mouth tastes sour. The sister's shoes are black, with spongy soles; the heels give slightly every time they make contact with the ground.

Inside the chapel of rest she turns to face us and we gather round. She indicates the door we should use. We can take our time, she says, her voice softening. She offers to hold the baby while Vivian is in the chapel, but Vivian shakes her head and says, 'She stays with me.'

I go first, struggling comically with a heavy curtain. Once I have parted the folds, I find myself halfway up a high-ceilinged room. Dad is below me, and to the left, on a raised bed. Two candles waver on a shelf above his head. I climb down the stairs, the others behind me, then walk over to where Dad is lying, his body draped in a weighty, embroidered cloth of blue and gold. I stand beside him, looking down. His mouth, which is covered with a swatch of muslin or gauze, has fallen open in a kind of sigh, and his lips have set in a position that makes him look oddly flirtatious. His eyes are closed.

The four of us circle the bed, Vivian still holding Greta. To begin with, we seem preoccupied with details: the small square of see-through fabric over his face, the white shroud in which his body has been wrapped. I am aware that I am looking at a corpse – my first – but I also know the dead person is my father. My mind oscillates between the two ideas; it just won't settle. Dad's neck is raw, discoloured, and I keep wondering how the rest of him has altered. There's a sense of the grotesque, of barely concealed horror. I remember what the sister told us on the phone. As a hospital, they lacked the skills of a funeral director, and we shouldn't expect too much. It would, she said, be fairly basic.

As soon as Vivian is satisfied that Dad is definitely dead – earlier, someone had suggested that she might use a pin – she climbs back up the stairs. Once she has disappeared through the curtain, Ralph approaches the end of the bed and touches the hill Dad's feet have made in the embroidered cloth. Seeming to follow Ralph's lead, Robin lays a hand on Dad's stomach. The three of us look at each other and smile, but there is a tension, a palpable uneasiness, as if we are expecting to be reprimanded and then asked to leave. I suddenly feel we are squandering an opportunity that is precious, unique. This moment will not come again. We should have agreed to visit the chapel one by one. We should all have had our own time with the dead man. But we are being governed by a group dynamic. We're still the little army I told Hanne about, full of bravado and hilarity, both of which are out of place. We're thinking not about our father but about each other.

I reach down and touch the hair above Dad's ear. It is cold. Dry. Brittle as spun sugar, it could snap or crumble in my fingers. I wish I could speak to him, but the presence of my brothers makes me self-conscious. My goodbye has to be a silent one. I have to think the things I should be saying. I try and send my thoughts through the air, from the inside of my head to the inside of his, but even though we're only a few feet apart, they fall short, glance off, or crumple, like paper planes thrown at a wall. This is wrong, all wrong. There is a moment when I nearly scream. I imagine how wild and mad it would sound, and how the chapel would reverberate, and how somebody in the hospital would hear me and come running. I imagine the looks on the faces of my brothers. I imagine my father's face too, motionless, unmoved.

Later, as we drive away, the pine trees closing in again, Robin blows some air out of his mouth and says, 'Thank God that's over,' but I feel I should be braking, turning round. I don't feel I've done what I came to the hospital to do, and yet I can't find it in myself to insist. Robin would object – or Ralph . . . I could always tell them to take the car, I suppose. I could make my own way back – a taxi to the station, then a train . . . But I don't stop until I reach the end of the drive, and then, once I have made sure nothing's coming, I signal right and set off down the hill.

Back in the house, I slip away from the others, climbing the stairs while no one's looking. In my hand is Dad's brown canvas-and-leather holdall, containing the things he took to the hospital with him. I open the door to the au pair's room. Darkness crowds the windows. There is a floral smell that reminds me of cheap hotels in Europe. A scent, I imagine, or a deodorant. All that remains of Forbes, who we will never see again. I realize I have forgotten her real name.

I shut the door and sit down, Dad's holdall on the bare mattress beside me. The zip parts to reveal his sheepskin slippers, offcuts of lurid green carpet glued to the soles for added insulation. Under the slippers I find his sponge bag. The contents are predictable enough: lavender soap, a flannel, throat pastilles, and so on. I turn back to the holdall. Beneath the sponge bag is the dark green tartan of his dressing-gown. As I push the dressing-gown aside, his hairbrush appears. Chipped wooden handle, one third of its bristles missing. I lift it to my nose. His smell is so vivid that it pushes at me like something solid, physical. Closing my eyes, I can almost believe he's in the room with me.

At the bottom of the holdall is a pair of neatly folded blue and white pyjamas. When I take out the jacket and hold it up, I see that something has spilled all down the front, leaving a ragged stain. It is blood. My heart thuds once, as if it just collided with my ribcage, and the breath stops in my lungs. I remember what Robin told me about Dad's death being peaceful. It doesn't look peaceful.

Dad would never use the word 'die' – at least, not about himself. He would always say, If something happens to me. Once, when I was fifteen, I heard him call my name. *Here a minute*. I found him downstairs, standing in the short passage that led to his study.

'What is it?' I said.

Dad stood at right angles to me, head lowered. 'I wanted to give you this.' He handed me a bracelet.

The two bands of age-blackened silver were carved with exotic designs in which I thought I detected either serpents or dragons. They were connected at one end by a hinge. At the other end were three tiny cylinders, which slotted into alignment when I brought the bands together. Attached to a miniature chain was a bolt, no thicker than a needle. Slide the bolt through the cylinders, and the bracelet would be securely fastened and couldn't fall off.

'It belonged to your mother,' Dad said. 'It was one of her favourite things.'

I threaded the slender bolt through the cylinders, wanting to summon her, but I didn't know what her arms looked like. I had no sense of the colour of her skin, or the texture, or the pattern her veins made underneath. The bracelet closed round a ghost wrist.

'Is it silver?' I asked.

'Indian silver.'

'Maybe you should keep it for me, in a safe place.'

'I want you to have it now,' Dad said, 'in case something happens to me.'

The words seemed to bruise my heart. 'Nothing's going to happen to you.'

'Well,' he said, his eyes lifting to the landing window.

'I don't *want* anything to happen,' I said.

Dad was still looking up into the stairwell. He would be thinking of my mother, Wendy, and how she had been taken from him.

The coolness of the hall. The dimness. Always a gloom in that part of the house, even in the summer.

Sitting on the au pair's bed, I stare at the black window. I try and make a list of things he loved. Boats. The sea. The poems of Dylan Thomas. Women with straight dark hair. Turkish delight. Cricket. Laurie Lee. Smoked haddock (he always called it 'yellow fish'). Smooth stones. Custard. Tongue.

The others are downstairs, in the kitchen. I can hear their voices through the floor.

In case something happens to me.

Well, now it has.

Laying Dad's pyjama jacket on the mattress, I lean over, press my face into the cotton. I stay like that for a long time, breathing him in, his last moments, his loveliness – everything he ever was.

Gravity Will Do the Rest

I met Fred, my future father-in-law, in December 1988. I had called from Frank and Miriam's house at four o'clock, telling Fred I was on the point of leaving, and that the drive would take about two hours. I arrived as six o'clock was striking. Fred answered the door. 'You're very punctual,' he said with a smile. My girlfriend, Kate, came downstairs a few moments later to find us standing in the hall, still chuckling. I told her that her father had just accused me of punctuality.

From the outset, and despite my odd get-up, which involved a bowler hat and a pair of Dr Martens, I felt that Fred accepted me. We lived in very different worlds – he was a professor of mechanical engineering at Liverpool University, and had also served as acting vice chancellor – but he was always eager to know what I was doing. And he was never intrusive or judgmental. He gave me the space to be myself. Sometimes, as I talked, I would feel his gaze resting lightly on me, benevolent, amused. Even early on, he seemed to love me unconditionally, like one of his own.

In 1998, Fred was diagnosed with prostate cancer. The following year, it metastasized into his bones. Returning from Italy with our baby daughter, and wanting to be close to Fred, Kate and I moved into a small cottage five miles from her parents' house. Fred's cancer didn't hurry, but by the summer of 2001 he was spending more and more time in Clatterbridge, an oncological unit on the Wirral.

On the first Sunday in September, Kate and I went to visit him. Lying in the boot of the car were the sweet peas Kate had picked that morning; I had watched her walk back to the cottage, her face lowered, the papery mauve-and-scarlet petals fluttering in her hand. As we drove west, towards the hospital, the trees that lined the road swayed in the wind, and white clouds jostled in the autumn sunlight, but the beauty of the weather seemed remote, gripped as I was by a dipping sense of apprehension, a tide of dread. Though Fred had fought hard, there was no hiding from the fact that death was near. We had learned the cruel truth about bone cancer. No one recovers. You cannot even hope.

When we entered the ward, Fred was sitting beside the bed. His ankles were swollen, almost purple. He appeared to be asleep. Kate kissed him on the cheek, then took his hand. He didn't open his eyes, but his fingers tightened around hers. She lifted the sweet peas until they were close enough for him to smell. Eyes still closed, he nodded. 'You're doing wonderfully well with your garden, my darling.' He didn't have the strength to function on our level for more than a few minutes at a time, but he was still the father he had always been, full of encouragement and admiration, full of love.

Later, he asked if I could take him to the lavatory.

'With your help, Rupert,' he said, 'I can do it.'

It seemed a privilege to be chosen for something so very personal. At the same time, I came close to tears.

In the toilet cubicle, I saw what a toll the disease had taken on him. That he should be reduced to this. Quite literally, reduced.

His knees were wider than his thighs.

Three days later, the staff at Clatterbridge agreed to discharge him, though they warned us he would need round-the-clock care. His wife, Jean, had a special bed set up in the dining-room.

The week that followed was filled with false alarms. On two or three occasions in as many days I was summoned from work, only to discover Fred wasn't about to die after all. I began to think that he would choose his moment, that he had his own private timetable for departure, though his suffering was becoming more and more unbearable, even to watch.

On the Friday, while I was visiting, he announced that he had decided to walk to his chair in the living-room. He was fed up, he said, with being stuck in bed.

'It's not a good idea, Fred,' I told him.

'I can do it,' he insisted, and began to try and hoist his right leg over the rail at the side.

'It could be dangerous. You might break something.'

'Not if you help me, Rupert. Just give me your arm. Gravity will do the rest.'

He was still such a man of science, even now, when he was so ill that he had all but lost the ability to speak. Once again, my eyes misted over.

Eventually, Jean and I managed to talk him out of it, and he sank back on to his pillows, exhausted.

The next day, Kate asked me to shave him. Though nervous, I agreed. I fetched his razor, some shaving-foam, and a bowl of hot water, then arranged a towel over his chest. I had never shaved anybody before, and worried I might cut him. The cleft in his chin was tricky, as was the groove beneath his nose. Tentative at first, I slowly grew in confidence. At times, I had the curious feeling that he had withdrawn far below the surface of his skin. He was like a man who stands at a window on the top floor of a house and watches someone working in the garden.

On Sunday morning, as I sat with him, holding his hand, he suddenly spoke.

'No hair on face,' he said in a hoarse voice.

I assumed he was referring to the fact that he was now clean-shaven, and was pleased he had noticed.

Pain had altered his appearance. His complexion was waxy, and his lips were thinner, almost feminine. His nose had sharpened. The creases defining his nostrils were deeper than before, so deep they looked black, and their curves seemed more pronounced, as if, in his illness, he had become fastidious, or even disgusted. It had been torture – I had heard him use the word when the district nurses moved him in the bed – but he had endured it without complaint, without self-pity. I sometimes felt the agony was purging him – suffering as a purifying force. He had arrived at a point beyond it – a place most people never reach. Our voices must have sounded so faint to him, our concerns so insignificant.

On Monday I had nearly an hour with him. I sat beside the bed, his hand in mine. Eyes closed, he seemed on the edge of unconsciousness, yet I was confident that he could hear me. I put my mouth close to his ear. I had always loved him as a father, I told him, and I had always believed that he had loved me as a son. I had learned so much from him; if I could be half the man he was, I would be satisfied.

I was proud to have known him. I would remember him for ever.

Once in a while, as I was talking, I would hear a soft sound in his throat or chest, and there were moments when he appeared to wince. It was as though he found this outpouring of emotion difficult to listen to, as though the mixture was too rich for him now that he was nearly gone, and I recalled what my godmother Ilaine had told me in 1984, and wondered whether I might be distracting him from his main purpose. Perhaps my words were weighing him down when all he wanted was to float away into the clear blue air.

'I'm sorry if it's too much,' I told him.

I was saying the kinds of things I had never been able to say to my father. Denied that one last chance to be with him, to speak to him, I had been left standing with my mouth open, dumbstruck, paralysed, even laughable, like somebody who tries to flag a bus down only to see it hurtle past.

'I can't help it, Fred,' I said. 'I'm sorry.'

As the feelings flooded out of me, I felt something coming back, not from him necessarily, but from somewhere, and it was stronger than anything I would ever be capable of, and it made me feel wonderful.

Parasites, Hangers-on and Layabouts

On the day of the reading of Dad's will, I drive downtown with Robin and Ralph. The sun keeps slipping behind big, torn rags of cloud; when we step out of the car, a brisk wind tugs at our clothes.

A shiny plaque – Levine & Levine – identifies the lawyer's premises. Once inside, we're ushered into a wood-panelled office by a secretary in a white blouse and a pencil skirt. We sit in a row on green leather seats. The room smells of carpet cleaner, and also, discreetly, of Parma violets.

Wearing a dark blue pinstripe suit and a pair of glasses that resemble Henry Kissinger's, Mr Levine begins by telling us how sorry he was to hear about our father. This is the language of death – automatic, unchanging, a little dog-eared – and we nod and smile, partly in recognition, and partly to let the lawyer know that he doesn't need to tread too carefully. We will not, for instance, be reaching for that adroitly positioned box of tissues on his desk.

Mr Levine tells us that he has been Dad's lawyer for

many years. Our father was, he says, 'a valuable client'. He tilts his head, and the light that filters through the net curtains behind us whitens the lenses of his glasses, making him seem momentarily nonplussed. His hair, which is naturally wiry, appears to have been forced into a side parting against its will. Looking down, he places his hands on either side of the document that lies in front of him, his fingers curled. The will is reasonably straightforward, he goes on. Our father has appointed us – myself, Robin and Ralph – as sole executors. His estate is to be split five ways, though such monies as our half-sister and half-brother, Rose Julia and Ryan Halliday, stand to inherit are to be put into a trust until they attain the age of eighteen. It will be our responsibility, Levine says, both to set up and to administer the trust. He glances up, anticipating questions.

'Ralph works in a bank,' I tell him.

'Most convenient,' Levine says.

He explains the concept of probate – once again, Ralph's employer will come in useful – then reaches for several sheets of writing paper that have been stapled together.

'There is also,' he says, 'a letter.'

The three of us exchange a glance.

I recognize my father's handwriting. The tops of his capital Rs are both rounded and elongated, like croquet hoops or shepherds' crooks, while the tails of his fs, ps and ys all lean backwards, as though a gale is blowing across the page. White spaces gape between each word.

'The letter is dated 30 October 1979,' Mr Levine says, 'and reads as follows: These are my wishes regarding certain of my effects and possessions in the event of my death. I desire that Rupert, Robin and Ralph together shall deal with my property with no others present, no parasites, no hangers-on or layabouts –'

The lawyer pauses, eyebrows raised, then surveys us over his thick black spectacle frames. As before, we nod and smile. He returns to the letter.

'I trust the three of you at all times to respect my wishes as regards Rosie and Halliday, who are to have their fair and equal share in fair proportion. I have done my best to bring you all up, give you a good home and education, try to see that you have learned to wash, eat properly –'

Mr Levine breaks off again and lays the letter on his desk. His right hand hovers over his unruly hair. 'I think perhaps it might be more appropriate,' he says, 'if you were to read this letter privately . . .'

Outside the lawyer's office, we loiter on the pavement, uncertain what to do next.

'Poor old Levine,' Robin says. 'He wasn't expecting that bit about the washing.'

That night I dream that I'm about to walk into the sitting-room. For some reason, though, I hesitate, and look to my left. In the gloom at the far end of the hall, I can see the front door with its upright letter box. My father's sheep-skin coat hangs on a hook nearby. The stairs rise towards the landing, their banisters varnished, treacle-black.

I face the sitting-room again, and this time I reach for the door handle. I feel its cool brass beneath my fingers as I press down.

When I step into the room, my father is sitting where he always sits, in his red chair. But there is something different about him, something I wasn't expecting.

'Dad?'

His corner of the room seems dark, the shadows deeper and more smoky than they ought to be, and I almost have to peer at him to make him out. I notice that all his clothes are wet.

'You're soaking, Dad.'

He glances down. He doesn't appear particularly distressed, or even surprised. He's simply taking it all in.

'You should change,' I tell him, 'or you'll catch your death.' This is one of his phrases, and I use it deliberately, hoping to get through to him. But he doesn't move. He merely says, 'Yes.' His voice is remote, disengaged.

'I'll fetch you some dry clothes.' But instead of climbing the stairs to the airing cupboard, I turn towards the French window that leads out to the garden.

The feeling I have on waking resembles regret, though it is weightier somehow, and murkier, more ominous. Dread seems to be involved, as if the dream isn't just a vision of my father, whom I have lost, or a reminder of my shortcomings as a son, but a warning, a premonition. It's as if the dream is showing me what lies ahead, as if there's something I can do.

But there's nothing I can do.

For the last seven years of his life, from the day Sonya left him to the day he died, my father lived alone. Sometimes he had au pair girls to cook, shop and clean for him, but since there were no children in the house, the agencies were becoming less obliging, more suspicious; it's not an au pair's job to keep an old man company. Dad was on his own for long periods, and occasional entries in his notebooks suggest he felt anxious and bereft, but it wasn't in his character to ask for assistance. There were not, in any case, many people he could have called upon. He had never believed in friendship. I don't understand why you need all these *friends*, he said to me once when I was about fifteen. For him, the family was all that mattered. But his first wife was dead, his second wife was gone, and his five children were scattered far and wide. The responsibility I feel in the dream is disturbingly familiar – it's how I felt during the years that followed my mother's death – yet it's a responsibility I fail to live up to. I don't help my father out of his wet clothes. I don't fetch a towel or try and make him comfortable. No, I turn away, towards the garden . . . Perhaps the dream is depicting the depression into which he is supposed to have plunged after Wendy died, or it might be showing me that he is dead, with water standing in for earth. Then again, in its portrayal of a certain resignation on his part, perhaps it is suggesting, as Ilaine did, that he is better off now, that he suffers less. Obviously, I would like to think so. But the truth remains. I didn't care for him. Nobody cared for him. Not at the end.

I drive north out of Eastbourne with Robin beside me. We're on our way to Gatwick Airport to collect Sonya and the children. Within twenty-four hours of hearing that Dad had died, Sonya told us that she wanted to attend the funeral, and that Rosie and Halliday were coming with her. After all, he was their father too, and it would be wrong, she thought, to exclude them from such an important moment in their lives.

As I enter the roundabout at Boship Farm, Robin brings up the subject of the films. While going through Dad's Super 8 home movies, we came across some footage of Sonya. In the first sequence she was walking down the stairs with nothing on, three white triangles shimmering behind the dark staves of the banisters. It must have been summer. The light in the stairwell had a kind of glitter about it, a gritty quality, as if the celluloid had been sprinkled with coal dust. A flash of black, a wobble, and Sonya was posing in the bedroom, still naked, the psychedelic curtains behind her. Then she was in the bath, the water shifting more slowly than in real life, and seeming denser, the colour rusty now, like the brown flakes that appear on a mirror once the silver has begun to decompose. The images were awkward, hard to believe in, almost supernatural. We only watched for a few seconds, then we switched off the projector and slid the reels of film back into their containers.

'How do we give them to her,' I ask Robin, 'without her knowing that we've looked at them?'

'We can't,' he says. 'We'll have to burn them.'

I wonder what these next few days are going to be like. I haven't seen Sonya since January 1977. Later that year, she moved back to Switzerland, taking the children with her, but before she left she wrote me a three-page letter in which she blamed me for the break-up of the marriage. She claimed I had never supported her. It would have helped if I had been more grateful, she said, if I had come towards her sometimes and embraced her, but I always pushed her away. *When I leave your father*, she wrote, *it will be him who suffers, not me.* That sentence had precisely the effect she must have hoped it would have: not only was it true – Dad *did* suffer – but it shifted the burden of responsibility back on to me, and this at the very time when I thought I might finally have broken free.

Not me. Was that true as well? It was something Sonya needed to believe, perhaps. She knew it wouldn't be easy to return to her home town and admit that her marriage had failed. But return she did. The years went by, and snippets of gossip reached us. *Sonya's working as a secretary. Sonya's fallen out with her mother. Sonya's seeing an ice-hockey coach. Sonya's drinking.* I didn't pay much attention to any of it. With two children to bring up on her own, though, and very little income, her life must surely have been a struggle.

She emerges from Arrivals in a black knee-length rain-coat that is belted tightly at the waist. Her hair looks darker, almost as dark as her coat, and her face is thinner, but she has the same jittery, sparkly quality about her, as if the atoms out of which she's made move faster and more impulsively than other people's. Distracted by the crowds and the announcements, Rosie and Hal haven't seen us yet. Sonya has, though. Her head tilts to one side, and there, suddenly, is the eager, slightly toothy smile I remember from all the photographs Dad took when they were first in love.

When Sonya arrived as our au pair in 1969, she was nineteen. I was only six years younger. I was already at boarding-school by then, and wouldn't have seen her except during the holidays. I never suspected that anything was going on.

After a year, Sonya flew home. My father wrote her letter after letter, telling her how much he loved her and how he could not envisage life without her. He begged her to become his wife. Sonya's family were horrified. She was still so young, barely twenty. The man courting her was more than twice her age, and partially disabled. He already had three children. There was no money to speak of. Where on earth was the future in that?

In 1971, just before Easter, Dad called me into the sitting-room. His eyes were paler than usual, and he seemed to be trembling all over, like a car with its engine running. He told me Sonya had written, saying she was coming back. He wanted to marry Sonya, he said, but he wouldn't go through with it unless we, his three sons, approved. Behind him, in the window, I could see Uncle Bert's house. Uncle Bert was the father of one of my closest childhood friends, and his garage smelled of the sugared almonds and dolly mixtures he stacked against the wall in big square silver tins. It always surprised me that somebody who worked for a company that made sweets could have such a nasty temper. Every time we jumped over the fence to retrieve a ball, Uncle Bert would yell at us for treading on his flower beds. Once, he even pelted us with bits of broken glass. We took our revenge by pouring half a bag of sugar into his petrol tank. Out of the corner of my eye, I saw Dad reach for his glass of water. He was still waiting for an answer.

Did I talk to my brothers? I suppose I must have. I imagine myself explaining that the marriage would be good for Dad, that he deserved it after all the terrible things that had happened to him, that it might be the only chance of happiness that he had left, and I can see Robin and Ralph, twelve and ten respectively, listening intently and glancing at each other now and then. Neither of them had any objections. Why would they? As an au pair, Sonya had been affectionate and lively, and she would be replacing a woman they couldn't even remember.

After a civil ceremony in the Town Hall, we celebrated with lunch at a Chinese restaurant called the Summer Palace. During the meal, Sonya gave off a kind of giddy radiance – her eyes flashed and glittered, reminding me of mirror-balls – and an Italian-looking waiter with slick black hair and a suave manner was particularly attentive, which soured the occasion for my father. He was a jealous man, even on his own wedding day. Sonya was excited by the prospect of her new life – we were all excited – though I did wonder how somebody who was only twenty-one could claim to be ready to settle down – to 'give up the bright lights', as she put it.

Perhaps because we were so close in age, Sonya was curious to know how much experience I'd had with girls. Once, when we were alone together in the car, she asked me if I had ever made love. I swallowed, then muttered, No. You must tell me all about it when you do, she said. She began to talk about sex, and how wonderful it was; her face appeared to flood with light. I looked away from her, wishing I could vanish through the floor. We were about to leave for the shops, or maybe we had just come back. I seem to see Dad's list in my hand: *Crusty white loaf, 4 oz tongue, yellow fish for one.*

When Sonya questioned me that day, I would almost certainly have blushed, not least because I'd just started going out with Larry Stevens, a boy at school. During the holidays, Larry and I wrote to each other constantly, and since our relationship took place outdoors, where we'd be less likely to be discovered, our letters were full of references to overgrown copses, unoccupied houses and disused signal boxes. Sonya had already noticed that I didn't bring girls home. Now she was becoming aware of the letters that thumped on to the hall floor three or four times a week, and always with the same writing on the envelope. In the mornings I would try and intercept the post, but when I reached the bottom of the stairs Sonya would often be standing by the front door, Larry's latest outpouring in her hand. So far as I know, she didn't open any of the letters, though I wouldn't have put it past her: her curiosity was such, I felt, that she would stop at nothing.

I was leading a double life, and the idea that I might be found out filled me with terror. I had already aroused the suspicions of my housemaster, a bulky, taciturn spin bowler from Yorkshire. One October night, Larry and I were out on the narrow road that circled the playing fields when I thought I heard the murmur of an engine behind us. I glanced over my shoulder. Just visible in the darkness was a car with no headlights on. I let go of Larry's hand, then told him to turn around and walk back the way we'd come. A few moments later, we passed a Mini creeping along in first gear, and there, hunched over the steering wheel, a trilby pulled down level with his eyebrows, was the grim but sheepish figure of our housemaster. It was at about this time that he took to calling me into his study. The shelves behind him crammed with books on adolescent psychology, he would tilt his Anglepoise lamp until it shone into my face and then embark on remorseless, hour-long interrogations. He would accuse me of kissing Larry Stevens. I would deny it. He would accuse me again. If I had been able to out-stare him, he might have believed me, but his eyes were a dark, dead brown, like old cricket balls, the sort you might find under a hedge, and I always ended up looking away. It was bad enough being under scrutiny at school. Now it was happening at home as well.

By the summer of 1972, Larry and I had split up. The following term, I fell for the daughter of a classics master. She lived in the school grounds, on an avenue lined with chestnut trees, and I often walked past her house, hoping for a glimpse of her. I will never forget the day the front door opened as I approached, and she appeared in a pair of white shorts, her blonde hair gleaming. The overhanging trees made a green tunnel of the road, and the light was dense and intimate. I tried to think of something to say. Nothing came. I was just moving beyond the house when she called out to me. Heart pounding, I swung round, only to see a Labrador shamble across the lawn towards her. Rupert, it turned out, was the name of her dog.

Since I still didn't have a girlfriend, I think Sonya assumed I was gay, and by the mid-seventies she had started to make veiled attacks on me at mealtimes. On one occasion, after a silence at the table, she announced that, in her opinion, homosexuality was an illness. I kept my head down and made a careful incision in a boiled potato. It wasn't natural, she went on. It was disgusting. My father agreed it wasn't natural. It was evil, Sonya said. My father thought this might be going a bit far. Leaning over the table, Sonya accused him of being against her. My father seemed baffled. He wasn't against her, he said.

'You always take their side,' she said, glancing at me, then threw down her knife and fork and whirled out of the room, slamming the door behind her.

I find it hard to remember much about that time, though there is one photo that helps to bring it back. I am reading a story to Rosie and Hal, both of whom are sitting on my knee. My hair is shoulder-length, and parted in the middle. This was 1975, and Robin had already left school. Since he now lived at home all year round, he witnessed the marriage beginning to disintegrate, and he would tell me about the quarrelling, Sonya brittle yet defiant, Dad gripped by an impotent despair. I only had limited experience of it myself. Once, while I was in my bedroom, Sonya began to scream hysterically somewhere below. I heard

Dad say, 'Stop it,' but she didn't. I jumped to my feet, then stood still, facing the wall. When Dad had told her to stop it eleven times, I put on David Bowie's *Diamond Dogs* and turned the volume up. I was scared these arguments might kill my father, but couldn't bring myself to intervene.

After graduating from Cambridge, I spent six months in America and Mexico, returning only days before my twenty-first birthday. How I wished I'd stayed away. By then, the fights had become frequent and vicious. Sonya had learned about the mental illness on my mother's side of the family, and was using it as ammunition. 'At least my children won't have any madness in them,' she said once, at lunchtime. I felt my insides knot with fury. When the meal was over, I took all the light bulbs out of the scullery cupboard, where Dad kept them, and hurled them, one by one, against the side wall of the house. A few days later, Dad emerged from the scullery, looking bemused. 'Has anyone seen the light bulbs?' he said. 'I'm sure I bought some.'

That winter I got a job at the Birds Eye factory, lifting tray after tray of cream cakes off a conveyor belt. By the end of my shift, I would be aching all over. Still, anything was better than being in the house. Sonya had been clamouring to go out at night – a meal in a restaurant, a show at the Congress Theatre – but Dad wanted her to sit at home with him. Play cards or watch TV. Go to bed early. I thought he was asking the impossible of her. She was only twenty-seven, after all. When I suggested that she might be feeling stifled, he looked away from me, tight-lipped.

'She chose this life,' he said. 'Nobody forced her.'

In three months, I had saved enough money to go travelling again. This time I chose Athens. Sonya was feeling so restless and trapped by then that I think she was envious of my forthcoming trip. She might even have thought I was deliberately flaunting my freedom. But I had dreamt of leaving Eastbourne for years, ever since I discovered there was a world beyond it.

While I was away, Sonya and my father separated. Sonya won the legal battle for custody, and then, in a decision he found unjust, not to say vindictive, she was granted permission to take Rosie and Hal to Switzerland with her to live. By the time I returned from Greece in the autumn, Dad was on his own. Throughout his life, he had appealed for peace and quiet, and those words had come back to haunt him: the silence in the house on Summerdown Road was a constant, pitiless reminder of the fact that he had lost his children.

I had only been home for a few days when he found a packet of raw jelly in the larder. I had just done the weekly shopping, and since he knew where everything belonged he was helping me to put the groceries away, but he had come to a standstill, with his back turned and his head lowered.

'Dad?' I said.

The jelly had been tampered with, he told me in an odd, strangled voice. At first he had suspected mice, but when he slid the jelly out of its packet he noticed a human bite-mark. Rosie had always loved jelly, he said. She must have crept into the larder one day when nobody was looking. His shoulders shook, and a tear appeared, round and black, on the stone floor of the larder.

'Dad,' I said again.

Stepping closer, I took him in my arms. I couldn't hold him too tight, though, or I would hurt him.

*

Eleven now, Rosie has grown, the top of her head level with her mother's shoulder, and she chats happily as we cross the airport car park, but Hal, two years her junior, scarcely opens his mouth. I am struck by his looks – of all of us, he is the one who most resembles Dad – but I also notice that he seems confused, distracted. Perhaps he is finding the English hard to follow; he isn't as fluent as Rosie, nowhere near.

On the journey back to Eastbourne, I let Robin do all the talking. Every once in a while I glance at Sonya in the rear-view mirror, her face in profile, angled towards the window, or lowered, shaded in, and my mind drifts back to the mid-seventies. At the time, I felt she targeted me unfairly, but now, a decade later, I have decided to put the past behind me, and I'm hoping she will do the same.

Turning into Victoria Drive, I accelerate up the hill towards the hulking silhouette of St Elizabeth's.

'So strange,' Sonya murmurs.

She will have recognized the church, and she will know, as I do, that we are only about a mile from home.

That night, when the children are in bed, we settle round the kitchen table with a bottle of red wine. Sonya soon becomes tearful, and I remember how a single glass would often be enough to make her tipsy.

'I had to come back,' she says. 'Just because things go wrong, it doesn't mean you forget how it was.'

'There were good times,' I say, 'weren't there?'

She nods slowly, dreamily.

I ask how it began.

'After three days,' she says. 'After three days he said, I'm in love with you.'

She wasn't in love with him, she tells us, but he didn't give up, and eventually she fell for him. They didn't sleep together, though, not while she was our au pair, not even once. 'I wanted to,' she says, 'but he said, No – not until we are married. I stayed in my room, and he stayed in his.'

She returned to Switzerland. After a year, she found she missed Dad – us too – and she flew back, and not long afterwards, while sitting on Dad's knee, she finally agreed to marry him.

She lights a cigarette, then looks round at the room, and her eyes blur in a kind of wonderment. 'So strange,' she says again.

She is back in the house, but he is gone. I wonder which fact is harder to believe.

'I still loved him,' she says later, 'even when it all went wrong.'

No one speaks.

She takes a drag on her cigarette and blows the smoke into the air above the table. 'I still love him,' she says, 'even now.'

Hanne rings early the next day. She tells me that she has had a call from a woman at the Olympiastadion. My hand flies up to my mouth. I completely forgot I was supposed to be starting a new job on the first of March.

In early February, while looking through the paper, I noticed an advertisement for a cleaning job at the stadium where Hitler's Olympics had taken place in 1936. I rang the number and secured an interview. The next day, I took the U-bahn to Spandauer Damm. I was to see a certain Frau Blücher.

As I left the U-bahn station, the stadium loomed out of the mist, bleak and forbidding, and I felt a quick, furtive thrill in the pit of my stomach. At the stadium gates, I asked for Frau Blücher and was directed to a flight of dank concrete stairs. I climbed down to the bottom, as instructed, and set off along a wide corridor that was lit by regularly spaced low-voltage bulbs. Behind one of the many doors, each of which was labelled in a mysterious, bureaucratic German that resembled code, I found Frau Blücher. The shapeless coat she wore over her clothes was the colour of charcoal, and her straight grey hair, which stopped just short of her ear lobes, had been cut so brutally that I imagined a pair of garden shears had been involved, or even, perhaps, a spade. She regarded me from across the room with considerable suspicion. Clearly I wasn't the sort of applicant she'd been expecting.

Lighting a cigarette, she asked me why I wanted the job.

'I'm writing a book,' I said. 'It's a dream of mine, to be a writer. But I need money.' I paused, trying to think of words that might tilt the scales in my favour. 'My German's not so good – you can probably hear that – but I can work hard.' I paused again, then added, 'I'm twenty-eight.'

'*Ein Schriftsteller . . .*' She frowned. 'No writing here.'

'Of course not,' I said, smiling. 'Anyway, my type-writer's at home, in Kreuzberg.'

It might have been a mistake to mention Kreuzberg, since it had a somewhat dubious reputation – people believed it to be riddled with anarchists, immigrants and other assorted scroungers, a belief that wasn't entirely without foundation – but Frau Blücher didn't appear to care. Stubbing out her cigarette, she informed me of the hourly rate. Perhaps she was hoping this might put me off. I just nodded, though, as if the figure was somehow

familiar to me, or unsurprising. She studied me for several
seconds, long enough for me to notice that one of her eyes
was bigger than the other. Now I thought about it, she
looked a bit like a Picasso.

'*Also gut*,' she said at last. 'You can start next month.'

When Hanne returned that evening, I told her the excit-
ing news, and we joked about the fact that she would now
be living with a *Putzermann* – a cleaner.

Sitting in Dad's chair, I stare at the blank side wall of
Uncle Bert's house. I had been looking forward to working
at the Olympic stadium. I had already pictured myself
underground, diligently sweeping. Imagine the thoughts
that would come to me, the conversations I would have!
The stadium was a world in itself, with its own unique rit-
uals and regulations, and I felt sure that it would provide
me with all sorts of extraordinary material – even, perhaps, a book. But now the job would go to someone
else . . . In not appearing at the beginning of March, I had
almost certainly confirmed Frau Blücher's initial opinion
of me, that I wasn't a serious candidate for the position.

'Was she angry?' I ask.

'I explained about your father,' Hanne says. 'She wanted
me to send – how do you say it?'

'Condolences.' I bring my eyes down from the window.
My father, this house – the months that lie ahead. 'I miss
you, Hanne,' I say. 'I miss Berlin.'

On the morning of the funeral, I wake up to see Robin
bent over the sink in the corner of the bedroom, vomiting.
I ask if I can get him anything. He shakes his head, then
retches. Watching as he grips the edge of the sink with
both hands, I remember Dad telling me how Robin kept

being sick on the day our mother died. The funeral is less than four hours away. I wonder whether he'll be well enough to go.

By midday, the vomiting has stopped, and he says he feels better. His eyes are bloodshot, though, and the colour has drained from his face. When he changes into his black clothes he looks more ghoulish still.

At half past one, the hearse arrives outside our house. Two other cars park close behind, their coachwork gleaming like patent leather. They have a sort of ceremonial bulk that seems out of all proportion to the road; should any of our neighbours still be unaware that Dad has died, they can hardly fail to notice now.

I walk out to the front gate. The air is chilly; I can smell wet leaves. On the pavement a tall, raw-boned undertaker in a black coat wraps his arms around himself against the cold. His black gloves make his hands look enormous, like a cartoon strangler, or Mickey Mouse. I tell him the rest of the family is on its way. He nods, then gazes off into the distance. His cheeks have a grazed look, as if it hurts him to shave. I face in a different direction. Sky the colour of exhaust fumes. I consider starting a conversation, but there's nothing to say, and I end up staring at the reflection of our legs in the car door.

Our speed doesn't rise above fifteen miles an hour, and the coffin remains in front of us, the blunt, blond end framed by the rear window of the hearse. *I love you all in different ways*, Dad wrote in the letter his lawyer gave us. *Your five lives have been my life, your joys and sorrows mine.* He carried me a little, without me feeling it, and that is what I have lost. Something as powerful and light as prayer. We turn down Church Street. Everybody on the pavement stops and stares.

In St Mary's the air is veiled, slightly opaque, as though made up of dust or sediment. Both sides of the church are filled with people we know. Frank and Miriam. Uncle Roland. Neighbours like the Goodchilds, the Martins. My ex-girlfriend, Tina. And Bernard too, of course. I look at Robin and Ralph, and they look back at me. Whatever binds us seems to tighten. We take our seats in the front row.

Organ music swells, and the coffin floats up the aisle on the pall-bearers' shoulders. As they draw level with our pew, one of them stumbles. The coffin lurches, dips, then rights itself, but not before I have imagined the toe end hitting the stone floor, the lid coming loose, and Dad's body sliding out, stiff as a canoe. I dare not glance at either of my brothers. I gaze at the ceiling instead, and bite my lip, and when I lower my eyes again, the pall-bearers have withdrawn, and the coffin is resting on a sort of trestle near the altar.

During the hymns we sing as loudly as we can. As in the chapel of rest, this is partly bravado, and we grin at each other between verses, but we are also venting some of our frustration and self-pity – it's like a kind of weeping – and by the time I leave the church and climb back into the big black limousine my voice is hoarse.

With the cemetery in sight, I suddenly realize that Sonya has no idea what is about to happen. In his will, Dad insisted that he be buried with Wendy, his first wife, and Sonya ought to have been forewarned, but somehow, with so much else to think about, none of us remembered. As our car glides between the high wrought-iron gates, I clear my throat and turn to her.

'Sonya,' I say, 'there's something you should know . . .'

When I have finished explaining, her face hardens, and she looks out of the window. I wonder whether it was Dad's intention to punish her from beyond the grave. Certainly, he never disguised his bitterness at her betrayal, which was how he thought of it, and he lost all faith in women as a result. You can't trust them, he would tell me. They say one thing, then do another. In his notebooks, he was still more virulent. Once, I stumbled on a page where he had written, *It's all take, take, take.* Then, further down, in a slanting, almost drunken scrawl, *All women are prostitutes.*

But no, I don't see it as revenge. It seems unlikely he would have involved Wendy in an act of recrimination that had nothing to do with her. Besides, he would never have imagined that Sonya would be standing at his grave-side; he thought of her as gone, for ever. Divorce has such a muddying effect. The end of his marriage to my mother may have been abrupt, but at least death is clean. There was no falling out of love with Wendy, no tarnishing of her memory – nothing to prevent the good times from rising to the top. I'm sure his desire to be buried with her was a pure one. He was looking for kindness. Returning to the place where he had felt most comfortable.

Not that this will be much consolation to Sonya. If I were her, I would feel snubbed. It's as though Dad is telling her that she never measured up. As though he is removing her from the story of his life. But after all, as Dad himself often said, she was the one who decided to leave, and she must have known him well enough to realize that he would never forgive her. He would often allude sarcastically to

Gotthelfstrasse, where Sonya lived after the separation. *God help her,* he would say. On her first night back, Sonya told us she still loved him, and I believed her, but a love like that wouldn't have made much sense to Dad. In his eyes, she had abandoned him, but worse than that, far worse, she had deprived him of his children. Though it's difficult to work out what else she could have done – apart, perhaps, from settling locally, in Eastbourne – the decision to return to Switzerland was cruel because it put them beyond his reach. Given the state of his lungs, flying was out of the question; in fact, Dad's doctors advised against long-distance travel of any kind. Every summer, Rosie and Hal would spend three weeks with him, and though he adored their time together, it would leave him physically and emotionally exhausted. Also, he saw how the children were growing away from him. He was becoming a kind of interlude in their lives, a habit that happened too seldom to be worthy of the name. They were losing their English; sometimes he would have problems making himself understood. He never felt his disability more than in those final years, and once or twice, when we were alone, he cursed it in language I had never known him use before.

At the graveside, I hear the clamour of young voices from the playground at the bottom of the hill. The two children are standing in front of me, and I look down at the tops of their heads. Is it appropriate for them to be here? Will it damage them? At the time of our mother's funeral, I was eight, and Robin and Ralph were five and three, and people felt it would upset us to attend. Later, when I asked Auntie Miriam about that day, she said she thought that she took the three of us up on to the Downs, and that we had a lovely time, just running about, 'being boys'. Though I have no memory of that, I can imagine it –

blue skies, a warm wind blowing, the town spread out below. *Look! There's our house!* We would have raced through the long grass, shouting, laughing, falling over. We might have pretended to be aeroplanes, with lots of engine noise and arms for wings . . . But then some upright lines appeared between Miriam's eyebrows, and she put three fingers to the corner of her mouth, and looking at me sidelong, almost slyly, said, 'But I remember being at the funeral . . .' She smiled at the foolishness – the treachery – of memory. One thing is certain, though: we didn't go. From one day to the next, our mother disappeared, and I don't think any of us understood what had happened to her.

I place a hand on Rosie's head. In a whisper, I ask her if she's all right.

She looks up at me, her lips pale, and she nods.

'Yes,' she whispers back. 'I'm fine.'

We heard somewhere that sherry is supposed to be served after a funeral, and we have bought a bottle of Harvey's Bristol Cream, which stands untouched on the kitchen table in front of the white wine and the cider. We're like foreigners, trying to observe the customs of a country that is unfamiliar to us. Someone asks if there is any tea. Vivian puts the kettle on, while I hunt around for cups and saucers.

Later, stepping out on to the lawn, I feel the damp ground through the soles of my shoes. Mist blurs the Downs; my hands are bloodless, cold. I walk up the garden, then stop in the archway and glance back towards the house. It has such a cheerless, run-down air. Did it always? Not in the sixties, surely. Not when we were young. Shabby, perhaps, and a bit chaotic, but never cheerless. In the last seven years, though, it has gradually fallen into a state of disrepair. The window frames cracked and rotted. Tiles slipped off the roof. The pebble-dash began to look grim, utilitarian. It became a house inhabited by a man who had lost almost everything, a man living a strange, abbreviated life, embittered and alone. My glass is empty. I move back down the garden.

Before I can reach the sitting-room, Uncle Roland intercepts me. As a child, I idolized Uncle Roland. He ran the Goodwood estate, which belonged to the Duke of Norfolk. Before that, he lived in Portugal. He was worldly, wealthy – everything my father wasn't. If anyone asked me what I wanted to be when I grew up, I would always say the same thing: a land agent, like my uncle. But then, during early adolescence, I became disillusioned with him; it was as if all the gloss and glamour dropped away, revealing somebody I neither recognized nor understood. At that age, I was intensely loyal to my father, and I suspect I began to side with him. The two brothers didn't seem to have ever been particularly close. Younger by four years, Roland missed the war entirely, and it is conceivable that my father resented his brother's good fortune. My father also claimed that Roland made light of, or even mocked, his disability. Whenever I saw the two of them together, which was only rarely, they would spend most of the time in superficial banter. Under this veneer of good humour, I thought I detected irritation, if not hostility.

Roland offers his condolences. He seems smooth, self-possessed, almost jovial. I have no sense of what he might be feeling, and find myself wishing he hadn't come.

The conversation shifts. He wants to know why I left

the advertising industry. Loathe to answer, I stare at my feet, but he pursues the subject.

'It was such a good career,' he says. 'You had real prospects. I just don't understand why you gave it up.'

I look into his eyes at last. 'I was making too much money,' I say.

He gazes at me in utter disbelief.

Back in the kitchen, I fill my glass with wine and gulp it down.

'What is it?' Ralph asks.

I shake my head. 'Nothing.'

Out in the garden again, I notice Tina standing by the fir tree. She is wearing a black sweater, and her thick blonde hair falls to her shoulders. We split up in 1981, not because we stopped loving each other, but because Tina thought she was too young, at twenty, to spend the rest of her life with me. She cried on the night she moved out. You'll never see me again, she said. You won't forgive me. I know you won't. I didn't say anything. I wanted to punish her, and the only power I had left was to withhold the truth. *Of course I'll see you. I won't be able not to. I love you.* We drove north, over the grim skeleton of Vauxhall Bridge. She was going to live with a friend from art college. I helped her carry boxes up the stairs and into her new bedroom. I didn't cry until I was back in my car. It was raining by then. As I entered the roundabout at Paddington Green, I nearly crashed into a van. Later, when I was home, I opened my notebook, but all I could come up with was a single, unsatisfactory line: *rain on the windscreen, tears on my face.*

She's as lovely now as she was when I first met her. I remember a holiday we had in Cozumel, and seem to glimpse her on our hotel balcony wearing nothing but the bottom half of a bikini she designed herself, the street below scattered with bits of palm tree from the hurricane that hit the island the day before we landed. I feel she was right to have broken up with me, and agree that there might have been restlessness or recrimination at some point in the future if we'd stayed together, but at the same time I suddenly regret having been so reasonable. I should have argued. Shouted. Thrown things. I should have told her I couldn't live without her. There are years we haven't had, countries we haven't seen. Perhaps that will never happen now . . . But as I watch her standing on the lawn, I sense there is something that can be revived, something that has still to run its course.

I walk towards her. She has driven down from London because she knew my father. He would tease her about all the make-up she used to wear. You don't need any of that, Tina. She would chuckle. Yes, I do. He would smile and shake his head. She didn't mind him being critical, perhaps because she realized that it was his way of telling her she was beautiful. In any case, he couldn't help himself; he liked women to look 'natural'. Oddly enough, that's how Tina looks today: scrubbed clean, as though she's just been for a swim. No hair dye or eye pencil. Not even any lipstick. When I reach her, she takes my arm and squeezes it.

'You've got no make-up on,' I say.

She gives me a guarded look, half hurt, as if she thinks I might be finding fault.

I smile at her. 'Dad would have approved.'

Eyes filling with tears all of a sudden, she tells me that she loved him.

'He loved you too,' I say. 'He really did.'

*

Robin and I are talking over by the hedge when Erica appears. Dad discovered Erica at the beginning of the seventies, when he developed an interest in genealogy. They have a grandfather in common. Erica comes from a branch of the family that emigrated to South Africa, but she moved to England when she was in her early forties.

'What are you two being so secretive about?' she says. 'Are you plotting something?'

'There's no need,' Robin says, 'not any more.'

He steers a look at me, and I feel sure he is thinking of the time we planned to do away with Dad. That night has stayed with me, mainly because it revealed an anger that I didn't, until that moment, realize was there, an anger rooted in his weakness, an anger which, like a flame in bright sunlight, only became visible if viewed from a certain angle.

Once, before I was born, my father had been strong, but a team of surgeons cut out most of the ribs on the right side of his body and then drained the fluid from his lungs with needles so thick that the diameter of the sharp ends could be measured with a ruler. When he was finally discharged from hospital, part of each lung had been closed down. He breathed faster and more shallowly than other people, and one half of his back sagged in such a way that his spine was thrown into unnatural relief. His scars had the muted gleam of silk or wax. One evening, while I was giving him his usual massage, he described what it was like to come round from a major operation. I felt as if I'd been flattened, he said. Run over by a steamroller. They gave him morphine to dull the pain. He became addicted. To break his habit, they simply halved the dose. The next day, they halved it again. He screamed for more. When I read Céline's *Voyage au bout de la nuit* and found the following sentence – *You can be a virgin in horror the same as in sex* – it was Dad I thought of first.

His years in hospital turned him into a different person. More fragile, less confident – a man who lived so prudently that his sons were almost guaranteed to throw caution to the winds. Sometimes he would stand in front of the basin in his bedroom, stripped to the waist, and he would talk about his sporting accomplishments, how he had rowed for his school, played rugby for the county. He would flex his right bicep. Look at that, he would say. Not bad, considering. He would invite me to feel the hard goose egg of muscle. Most parents want their children to be able to imagine them as they once were, in all the careless glory of their youth, but for my father there was so much more at stake. In his twenties, he had been brutally altered, savagely diminished, and he was desperate for me to see him as he used to be, as he was *supposed* to be – as he *truly was*. But I never could. I never could.

Given his injuries, he did well to last until he was sixty-one. At the hospital, the sister told us that he had been living on borrowed time, and I wondered to what extent his survival had to do with us, his children. *Your five lives have been my life.* Since his death, we have been joking about our new status as orphans, but if I go back twenty years, that was a very real possibility. It was also my greatest fear. My mother, who was young and healthy, had been taken. My father was still with us – but for how much longer? From the age of eight, I would lie awake at night and pray for my father not to die. My bedroom shared a wall with his, and if he murmured in his sleep, or even if his mattress creaked as he turned over, I would freeze, heart thudding, afraid his lungs had filled with fluid. Once, when I was nine, Dad woke to hear water running in the upstairs bathroom. He looked at the clock. It was late – after two. He stepped out on to the landing. My eyes wide open, I brushed past him as if he wasn't there. I sleep-walked through the house that night, turning on every tap I could find, and Dad followed me from room to room, turning them all off again.

My prayers were answered – Dad didn't die – but the effort I had to make night after night produced a smouldering resentment. I wished he could be like other fathers. I hated having to worry. I longed for a life that was selfish, nonchalant, carefree. Why should I have to bear the brunt of all this terrible uncertainty? Why me?

Erica has given up trying to extract our secrets, and she is facing away from us, one gloved hand cradling the other. 'We didn't see each other very often,' she is saying, 'but we talked on the phone. We were always talking on the phone . . .'

'He didn't see anyone very often,' I say.

She keeps her eyes fixed on the end of the garden for a moment longer, then abruptly, almost defiantly, turns to me. 'I'm going to miss him, you know.'

She touches the back of a glove to her right eye. A tear darkens the leather. Watching her, I wonder if she might not have been a little in love with Dad.

Before flying back to Switzerland, Sonya asks about the house. She seems to believe that if we put it on the market Rosie and Hal will be entitled to a share of the proceeds. When I correct her, she gives me a suspicious look, and though I'm sure she must have heard the story before, I tell her again.

My maternal grandfather, James Gausden, bought the house shortly before the start of the Second World War, I say, and when he died in 1948, it passed to his wife, Pim. A year or two later, Pim was admitted to a mental institution in Northampton, where she was diagnosed as a chronic diabetic and a manic-depressive. The house, known as 'Rokkosan', stood empty until 1953. Meanwhile, Pim's daughter, Wendy, had met my father, and they had fallen in love. With a wedding planned, but unable to afford a home of their own, they asked Pim whether they could move into Rokkosan, at least until she felt well enough to return. She gave her permission, adding that she had no intention of returning.

On Pim's death, in the early seventies, her will was found to be simple and uncontroversial. Her estate was to be divided equally between her three children, Frank, Joe and Wendy. Since Wendy was already dead by then, and had died intestate, her share of the assets devolved directly to her children – Robin, Ralph and me. A valuation of the house revealed it to be the rough equivalent, in cash terms, of one third of everything Pim owned. It was decided that we should inherit the house as our share of our grand-mother's will, which meant that we wouldn't have to find somewhere else to live.

'The house never belonged to Dad,' I tell Sonya, 'not even thirty years ago, when he moved in. It belonged to his mother-in-law, and then to Robin, Ralph and me.'

But Sonya is shaking her head. I imagine she simply doesn't want to believe what she is hearing, and who can blame her? When she first discovered that the house in which she was living, the house in which she hoped to raise her children, didn't belong to her, and never would, and that she could, in theory, be evicted at any moment, she must have felt as if the ground had quite literally dropped from beneath her feet. She must also have nursed a sense of injustice. I seem to remember talk of Dad and Sonya moving – this would have been in the mid-seventies – though nothing ever came of it.

'Sonya,' I say, 'it's true.'

Still shaking her head, she stares at the kitchen window, which streams with condensation, and it comes as no great surprise when we discover, two weeks later, that she has hired a local lawyer to monitor our handling of Dad's estate.

Once Sonya and the children have gone, we divide into two separate camps – myself and Robin on the one hand, and Ralph, Vivian and Greta on the other. Since Ralph and Vivian never seem to do anything as individuals, we have started calling them 'the Unit'. Of the little army that existed prior to the funeral there is no trace.

Moving through the house, I begin to notice spaces. On mantelpieces or windowsills. In drawers. I keep thinking, There used to be something there – didn't there? I feel the lack of things I cannot name, or even picture.

One morning, I find Robin in the scullery, hovering over the stove. Dressed in a black and white herringbone coat he bought second-hand in Aberdeen, he is stirring the contents of a saucepan. His size-twelve Dr Martens shuffle on the lino. I peer past him, into the pan. Chunks of something that could be potato float in a dingy brownish-yellow slurry.

I lean on the sink and gaze at the dustbins. As usual, they are full to overflowing. The dustmen have told us to contact the council and make what they call 'special arrangements', but Robin and I have decided to make some 'special arrangements' of our own: from now on, we're going to burn all our excess rubbish in the kitchen garden.

I face back into the scullery. 'I'm not sure if I'm right or not,' I say, 'but I think things are disappearing.'

Robin looks at me over his shoulder. 'Like what?'

'It's hard to say. It's hard to notice things when they're not there any more.' I pause. 'Like that time you came home for Christmas with your eyebrows shaved off and Dad couldn't tell what was different about you.'

Robin chuckles. 'I remember that.' Then, after a while, he says, 'You mean, things are being taken . . .'

'Maybe – but who by?'

'Not me.'

'Not me either.'

I believe him, and I can tell that he believes me – but then I would hardly have brought the subject up if I were guilty. I stare at the small square window above Robin's head. Outside, the wind rushes against the house. The broken plastic ventilator spins.

Robin's eyes narrow. 'The Unit.'

'Or Sonya,' I say, 'when she was here . . .'

'She was always going off by herself, wasn't she – into rooms . . .' Robin gives his food one last stir, then switches off the gas and moves the saucepan on to the blue work surface next to the stove. 'But you can't actually think of anything?'

'No. It's just a feeling.'

'The Unit, though – there's no telling what they've got squirrelled away behind that locked door of theirs.' Robin stoops over the pan. From where I am standing, all I can see is a pair of elbows and a big curved back. Is it a heron he reminds me of? I'm not sure. In any case, it's all over in a couple of minutes, and he turns, wiping his mouth on the back of his hand. 'Is it Thursday tomorrow?'

I nod.

'The Batcave's on Thursdays,' he says.

'That's a thought.'

He dumps his empty saucepan in the sink.

'What was that, anyway?' I ask.

'Curry,' he says.

The next day Robin and I set off up the A22 in Dad's Renault, arriving in the Oval at about six. The grainy air, the dusty trees; the gas-holders burnished by a low orange sun. We look at each other and smile. London again. London at last.

As we pull into the courtyard, a bulky woman lurches across the tarmac in a blue plastic raincoat. She lives in a flat on the fourth floor. Her legs are always bare, even in winter. I shout hello.

'All right?' As usual, she sounds as if she's got a cement-mixer for a larynx.

'I'm fine. How's your husband?'

'He's all right.' She calls her husband 'Dad'. I used to hear her yelling on the stairs. *You coming, Dad? I haven't got all bleeding day.*

I ask Robin whether he has ever seen her cross the road. He doesn't think he has. She doesn't bother with traffic lights, I tell him, or zebra crossings. Instead, she launches herself off the kerb, rocking from one leg to the other, like the pendulum from some lurid nightmare of a clock. Any cars that happen to come along have to brake and let her past. Once, a lorry driver had the nerve to give her a blast on his horn. Her great head swivelled. *Fuck off*, she growled at him, and just kept going.

'That's what I love about living here,' Robin says.

The building is a C-shaped thirties' council block, with concrete walkways that run the length of each floor. At night, when spotlights angle down into the courtyard, it feels like a prison. We lock the car and start up the draughty stairs. There are the habitual, pungent smells of urine and fried food. I no longer have a key, but Robin lets us in. The flat looks pretty much the same as it did when I lived in it with Tina. Vivid orange kitchen, blue bathroom. Synthetic tartan carpet in the lounge. When I left the country in 1982, I asked Graham, a friend of mine, if he would like to move in. A few months later, Robin took over my room. Since then, they have been joined by another mutual friend called Chris.

In the kitchen, Robin opens a can of Special Brew. I reach past him for the kettle. The NSU I caught from a ballet-dancer in Amsterdam three years ago has flared up again – the doctor said it might recur in times of stress – and since I have been put on antibiotics I'm not supposed to drink. I make myself a cup of Nescafé instead.

Before too long, a key turns in the lock, and Chris walks in. He is wearing what he always wears – black T-shirt, black trousers, and a pair of black Lonsdale boxing-boots. Chris works as an art director at a small advertising agency in Soho. We refer to him as Kennedy because he is always getting himself assassinated – by alcohol, usually, or drugs.

'Oh God,' he says when he sees us. 'Trouble.'

We pummel him in the ribs and stomach. He pushes us away. Settling on a beanbag, he pulls the ring on a can of beer, then takes out a packet of Silk Cut. We ask where

Graham is. He runs a hand through his hair; his big, pale face stirs dreamily. He doesn't know. When Chris looks at you, his eyes are so dark and blank that it's easy to imagine he is blind. We tell him the Batcave is on tonight. Does he want to come?

'Not if you two are going,' he says.

We ready ourselves for the club. I wear my black calf-length oilskin, as always. My eyelids are ghostly with greasepaint, and I've darkened the lower rims with kohl. Robin has used the kohl as well. His sixteen-hole Doc Martens and baggy mohair jumper are topped off with a crude gel-fierce blond Mohican that he gave himself a few nights back.

By ten o'clock, we're walking north on Carnaby Street. We push through a chipped black door, then up a narrow, creaky flight of stairs. Our teeth whiten in the ultraviolet. We hand our entrance money over. Once in the club, we head straight for the bar. The place smells toxic, chemical: hairspray, hydrogen peroxide, cigarettes. I order tonic with lime juice. Music lunges from tall black speaker stacks – the churning chainsaw snarl and vicious bass thump of an Alien Sex Fiend track. The sound's so loud it feels solid; you can almost lean against it. We breathe in deeply. This is what we've missed. Exactly this.

Since I'm not drinking, I'm going to do amphetamines. Well, I probably would have done them anyway. I scan the room for Wembley. There he is, runt-short, needle-thin, skulking in a fog of dry ice near the toilets. I call him Wembley because his hair stands up all round the edge of his head like football terraces. The shaved patch in the middle is the pitch. I don't know his real name.

'Wembley?' I shout over the music. 'You got any speed?'

He gives me his usual look – a blend of anxiety, cunning

and exasperation. 'Of course I've bloody got speed. What else would I be doing in this dump?'

A fiver buys me what I need.

I take Robin into the Ladies. We lock ourselves in a stall and chop lines on top of the cistern.

'Fucking hurry up,' a girl says through the door. 'I'm desperate.'

Back at the bar, I order another tonic-and-lime. My heart begins to rattle like a stone in a tin can. The drugs are kicking in.

A French girl asks me for a cigarette. Blue light skids off her cheekbone as she inhales. She moved to London a few months ago, she tells me. She works in a shop in Covent Garden. Her name's Monique. I offer her a line. In the harsh glare of the toilets she looks even prettier, a quarter-smile on her lips, her short blonde hair tousled, dirty-looking.

'Not you again,' says the girl who was desperate before.

The house band, Specimen, appear on stage. They slouch, spindle-legged, over their instruments, but there is nothing casual about the sound. The drummer starts out on his own, each beat emphatic, a crisp but savage detonation, white light flash-bulbing off his silver kit. In comes the bass, which twangs and snaps, springy as a blown-up rubber band, and lastly a brooding, rumbling guitar with a nasty edge to it, like the kind of jagged metal that gives you tetanus. They're playing their most famous song, and everybody's on their feet. The dance floor bounces.

At closing-time, I clatter down the stairs and out on to the street. Robin's already there. We decide to walk back to the flat. I check the knot of people on the pavement, but the French girl's gone. It doesn't matter. She's told me where she works. And nothing could have happened anyway, not with the disease I've got.

Through Soho, its streets medalled with chewing-gum and spit, drunk people staggering. A curtain of multi-coloured plastic strips gapes suddenly. Fuzzy disco beats, a woman beckoning. Down Charing Cross Road, shop doorways clogged with the slumped shapes of the home-less. On through Trafalgar Square. Some bare-chested idiot is splashing about in the fountain. It's cold, but he can't feel a thing. He's bellowing 'Stand and Deliver' by Adam and the Ants. Down Whitehall, over Lambeth Bridge. The river stretches below us like a sheet of wrinkled black plas-tic. Like a bin bag. A right turn, past the Imperial War Museum.

By the time we walk in through the front door, it's five in the morning, and Graham is already up.

'Guys,' he says.

Graham has a rosy complexion and thick, shiny hair, and his voice is soft but urgent, with an American blur to the vowels, as if he might once have lived on the West Coast. We tend to think of Graham as a sort of hippie. The twisted end of the sixties, though. Not Woodstock. More like Altamont. There is something unstable, even maniacal, about the grin he often carries on his face. In November, when I last stayed in the flat, an oblique psychological battle was being fought between Graham and Robin. Robin would be trying to extract an admission from Graham, the simple acknowledgement of a truth that ought to have been obvious, but Graham would sidestep Robin's probing, or simulate amused bewilderment, or sometimes, like a mirror, he would answer Robin's questions with questions of his own – What's your *problem*, Robin? What do you *want* from me? – and always in that infuriating, phoney San Francisco accent. The verbal skirmishing would go on for hours, and in the end Graham would frustrate Robin to such a degree that Robin would attack him physically. When Robin had him pinned to the floor and was threatening to hit him in the face, Graham would be gloating. Robin had been the first to crack. Robin had resorted to violence. Look, guys, Graham seemed to be saying, he's really lost it this time.

I settle on the carpet, with Robin to my left. Graham is sitting on my grandmother's sofa. He has made himself a cup of herbal tea. Behind me, the sash window is open, and cold air pushes against my back.

Our conversation revolves around recent events in Eastbourne. Robin and I know all about death now – we're experts on the subject – and since we've had a gram between us, we do most of the talking.

'It wouldn't be so bad to die,' Robin says.

I'm nodding. 'We've seen it up close now. There's nothing to be afraid of.'

Graham sips his tea. 'So why don't you do it then?'

'Do what?' I say.

'Die.' He is grinning, but his pale eyes look ruthless, volatile.

In November, I discovered that although Graham had been subletting my flat for a year, he had paid no rent at all. He has also been wearing my clothes, and he has lost the Savile Row waistcoat my mother gave my father in the fifties. It's possible he is testing me. How much can he get away with? What will it take to make me react?

'Hey,' Graham says. 'There's a window right behind you. You could throw yourselves out of it right now.' He isn't laughing. He isn't even joking. He's going to try and talk us into committing suicide. 'There's the window, guys,' he says. 'If you're not afraid of dying, why don't you jump?'

We glance at the open window, then at each other.

Robin shakes his head. 'Look, fuck off, Graham,' he begins, but Graham talks right over him. 'Jump. Go on.' Then he uses our own words. '*It wouldn't be so bad.*'

The window yawns, and I feel I'm being drawn backwards. The same thing happens when you lie on your stomach and peer over the edge of a cliff: your legs seem to lift behind you, tipping you towards the void. I feel I might be about to leap to my death despite myself. Is it happening to Robin too? I don't dare look.

Graham's grin has tightened, and his eyes are chips of grey glass in his ruddy face. 'Go on, you fuckers. Jump.'

Laughing quietly, I stare at the carpet. I do my best to ignore the air shifting behind me. I have to pretend the window isn't there.

'You're full of shit,' Graham says. 'Both of you.'

He goes out to the kitchen.

Later, driving out of London, we can poke fun at Graham and his little games. It's rush hour, and all the traffic is going the other way. We have wound the windows down. We've got our sunglasses on. We're full of shit.

'He really wanted us to do it,' Robin says.

'I know,' I say. 'He's jealous.' I'm not sure what I'm saying – it just came to me – but it seems like a good theory. 'He wants to *be* us,' I go on. 'He *hates* us. He wants to destroy us.'

I have just remembered the night I brought a new girl-friend round to the flat for the first time. As we sat on the tartan carpet, smoking a joint, Graham turned to Natalie and said, I bet you've got a nice cunt, haven't you?

'You know, I don't think you should stay there much longer,' I say. 'I think he's got it in for you.'

'I'm not going to,' Robin says. 'When we're finished in Eastbourne, I'm going to get a place of my own.'

'Good. That's a good idea.'

'I'm not going to live with a fucking maniac.'

'I don't blame you. I wish I'd never said he could move in.'

'He's always got that grin on his face. He does it deliberately. I wish he'd stop grinning.'

'Me too.'

'I mean, he's not happy, is he?'

'Fuck, no,' I say. 'He's furious.'

Robin bursts out laughing.

Just after seven, to the north of Uckfield, we surge over the crest of a hill. The speed is still working; my mind feels streamlined, customized. On our left is Nutley Heath and the western edge of Ashdown Forest, a landscape at once familiar and magical: pine trees with feathered dark green branches, patches of sandy soil in among the gorse.

As we start down the long descent, the heath on both sides now, I press the accelerator. Eighty, eighty-five. Speed and speed – and the desire for some sort of breakthrough, access to a new level. Ninety. To keep accelerating till you burst through an envelope, and suddenly all the noise and chaos falls away, and everything just floats.

'How fast are we going?' Robin shouts above the roar of the wind.

I check the speedometer. 'Ninety-five.'

A smile on his lips, he leans his head against the back of the seat and shuts his eyes.

*

That week, I move into what we think of as the au pair's room. Once it was Sonya's, of course, during the year that she stayed in her room and my father stayed in his. Then, for the seven years their marriage lasted, it was Ralph's room. Later, when Sonya had gone, it became the au pair's again. Though small, it has two windows, one with a view of the back garden and the Downs, the other overlooking the white mock-Spanish house next door. I have a single bed and a chest of drawers. There is also a pink wardrobe, made of plywood, where the au pairs used to hang their dresses. I like the room for its simplicity, and because it has no history for me; I never slept here as a child.

A protocol emerges. Robin and I sleep late, allowing the Unit to have their breakfast uninterrupted. Ralph has talked the bank into transferring him to one of its smaller branches in Brighton, and he now spends far less time commuting. As soon as he has left for the station, Vivian shuts herself in Paradise with Greta, and Robin and I don't see her after that. Sometimes we're not even sure whether she's in the house at all. If I happen to come across her – in the hall or on the landing – she just looks at me and doesn't speak, and I think of the night I arrived, and how she reminded me of a cat staring at a pointing finger. Is she afraid of us, or actively hostile? Or is she merely shy? These aren't the kind of questions you can ask.

I spend a morning in the garden, raking the flower beds. Some of the leaves have been lying on the mud for so many months that they have turned black. They give off a bitter, vinegary smell. I pick one up. It feels like a wet mirror; my fingers almost skid on it.

I fork the leaves into the deep metal wheelbarrow our

gardener used to give us rides in when we were young. His name was Mr Moore, and his hair was rust-coloured, wiry as the springs in sofas. Even though he had no teeth, he could still eat apples; he used his gums to bite them up. Once I have filled the barrow, I push it into the kitchen garden and tip the leaves on to the compost heap, then I swing round to collect another load. I remember how Mr Moore's arms were tattooed with anchors and serpents from his years in the merchant navy. Sometimes he would mention ports he had visited – Hong Kong, Mombasa, Veracruz – and his eyes would go as hazy as pieces of horizon.

Towards midday, I climb my favourite sycamore, its bark rumpling where the branches meet the trunk, like sweaters when you push the sleeves back to the elbow. I peer over the fence into Uncle Bert's garden. Some years ago, they found him lying dead next to the machine he used for turning the soil. Still switched on, it was tearing frantically at the earth, as if it had got it into its head to dig a grave for him. A breeze picks up; the sycamore shifts. As a boy, I used to lower myself off the tree on to the top of the laurel hedge that grew next to the fence. I would float face-down, high above the ground. Swimming on that sea of leaves, exhilaration would fill my body like a colour or an ache. Dusk. A blackbird spilling notes into the air. The kitchen window glowing, the distant clatter of a saucepan lid. The shape the light from the house made on the lawn. I remember a feeling that was like nostalgia, but it was rooted in the present, a time I was still inhabiting, as though I somehow knew it was already passing, nearly gone. Perhaps it was a foretaste of how I would feel in the future, when I looked back, or perhaps I had an intimation of how fragile things were, and how they were about to change for ever.

I drop out of the tree, then push through the gap between the hedge and the side of the glasshouse, and find myself in a narrow, grassy passage, the wall of Uncle Bert's garage to my right, our sitting-room to my left. I look up. Above me is the window of the dressing-room, where Greta sleeps. At night, when I was ten, I would lean on that sill and stare over the darkened gardens to the ghostly thumbprint of the chalk pit, and the black ridge of the Downs beyond. It was in that part of the house that I spent hours praying for my father to stay alive. It was in that part of the house, years later, that Tina and I first went to bed together. But now Ralph and Vivian have locked me out. They might almost be trying to tell me that there are areas of my life I have no access to.

As if I didn't know.

I round the corner, cross the small front lawn. When I reach the drive I pause again. It was here, on a hot, still afternoon in 1965, that I heard my mother call my name, though she had died the year before. I look at the yew tree with its drab berries, then I turn my gaze on the upstairs windows, as blank now as they were then. I see myself on the day it happened, my face pushed deep into the counterpane, my grandmother standing over me. Beyond us, the callous beauty of the evening sunlight. Strange how the world could turn away from you, how it carried on regardless. You meant so little to it.

I lower my head, but feel nothing except a rapid, gentle oscillation, as though a humming-bird is trapped inside me. The tap of footsteps on the pavement. A car flashes past, and then another. Was the sound of my name a reverberation, an echo of the countless times my mother must have called me? Or was it a sign of my desperate, hidden need for contact? I don't know. All I can be sure of is, I never heard her voice again. The air around me swirls. I have the sudden sense that I might levitate.

As I move towards the front gate, I swallow once or twice. I stand on the pavement, hands in pockets, looking up and down the road. It will be like this tomorrow, and next week, and in a hundred years. There's nothing for me here.

I see our neighbour, Jenny Martin, leave her house and walk into the garage. As she unlocks her car, she glances sideways and notices me. I give her a small wave.

'Do you need a lift somewhere?' she calls out.

Under Uranus

In September 2005, I decided to visit Auntie Beth, my mother's cousin. Beth and Wendy had been close friends, especially during their teenage years. Other people might have known my mother better, but no one had Beth's recall or her way with words.

A few days before setting out, I called Beth for directions. I hadn't seen her since the early nineties, and could no longer remember where she lived. The phone must have rung fifteen or twenty times before I heard her on the other end. She apologized for taking so long to answer. Her cat slept on top of the phone, she said. He didn't react when it rang because he was deaf. She gave me detailed instructions on how to find her house – a pub, a cattle-grid, a wood of larch and beech trees – all of which I jotted down, then asked whether I would be staying the night. I told her I'd like to, if it wasn't too much trouble. She'd have to move the ironing, she said. Perhaps I could bring a blanket, otherwise I might not be warm enough. 'I'm not suggesting,' she went on with a chuckle, 'that you get in with me.'

I left London at one o'clock with a bunch of lilies on the back seat, and by half past three I was passing through the wood Beth had mentioned on the phone. She lived on her own in a three-storey property that was buried, like a Mayan pyramid, in a jungle of foliage and brambles; from the unpaved road, all I could make out was a triangle of grey roof in the tangled mass of green below. The name of the cottage was painted on a piece of cardboard that leaned against a hedge, but the latch-gate beyond the garage was stuck fast. I jumped over, then picked my way down a steeply sloping garden, only to emerge on to the drive of the house next door.

'What on earth do you think you're doing?' A blonde woman bustled towards me with flushed cheeks.

'I'm looking for my Auntie Beth.' I waved the bouquet, evidence of my good faith.

The woman's indignation faded. 'Sorry, but we get some odd characters round here.' She told me it would be best if I returned to the road. The steps leading to my aunt's house were just to one side of the garage door.

As I climbed back through the wild garden, it struck me as entirely fitting that Beth should be so elusive. Our family was full of relationships that had been neglected or overlooked and were now lost to view.

This time I found the steps. Starting down towards the house, I could see a cement porch ahead of me, its side window jammed with cardboard boxes and plastic bags. The muddy ground near the back door was littered with cooked spaghetti, carrot stumps and rashers of bacon, and I remembered what Miriam had said when I told her I was going to visit Beth. *You know what it's like, don't you?*

I paused on the threshold to the kitchen. Every available

surface was heaped with cans, tins, packets and cartons. Near the stove, on the floor, stood a mound of fresh produce. It was three or four feet high, and most of it was good quality, from either Sainsbury's or Waitrose. A column of tiny fruit flies spiralled in the air above, as if illustrating the structure of DNA. Against the wall were the deaf cat's food bowls, four of them, none empty. There were two narrow passageways between the stacks of groceries: one led to a dresser and then turned right, into the living-room, while the other branched left, allowing access to the cooker and the sink. During my previous visit, Beth's fridge had been so full that food had avalanched on top of me when I opened the door. Things seemed to have got a bit worse since then.

'Beth?' I called out.

'Is that you?'

Beth appeared at the far end of the kitchen in a pink sweater and black slacks. Though her hair had whitened at the front, I recognized her wide eyes and her oddly permanent grin. She somehow managed to look startled and kindly, both at the same time.

We gave each other a hug.

'You haven't changed, Beth.'

'Oh, I *have*.'

She put the kettle on, then arranged my lilies in a vase. I noticed that her hands shook violently, and asked whether she was all right. She told me that her nerves had been affected by her diabetes. If she drank anything, she had to use a straw, she said, still grinning, or it went everywhere. But you've seen a doctor, I said. Oh yes, she replied. She gave me the flowers to carry, and a lardy cake to go with my cup of tea, then showed me into the living-room.

'I've cleared a space for you,' she said.

Stopping behind her, I let out an involuntary gasp. Usually, when people say they have cleared a space for you, they mean they have tidied away a few magazines or plumped up a cushion, but Beth was being literal. The rubbish in the living-room was hip-high throughout. Since it was mostly paper, the predominant colour was white, but mingled in with it were items as various as hot-water bottles, shampoo, a cordless hedge-trimmer, some Christmas decorations, a Wellington boot, and a can of Guinness. In this room, as in the kitchen, there were pathways. One was L-shaped, and led to the wood-burning stove, while a second cut directly across the room to the bay window on the far side. Halfway along the second path was a kind of offshoot that veered to the left. This third path served no other purpose than to allow Beth to reach her chair, which was covered with crocheted blankets and pages from a tabloid newspaper. The chair's position at the end of what amounted to an aisle gave it a stately air, not unlike the seat of an oracle, or a throne. Above the fireplace, and gazing impassively out over the scene, were several mounted kudu heads.

Once I had put the lilies on the windowsill, I sat down in the space Beth had cleared for me, which was one half of a green velour chaise-longue. I told her I couldn't remember when I had last seen her. She asked if it was in the summer. I said I didn't know. I thought Robin had been with me, though.

She surveyed the banks of paper that surrounded her. 'I expect it wasn't quite like this.'

'Well, no,' I said.

We both laughed.

'The last time Robin came, he offered to take some of it to the dump, but I told him not to worry.' Beth gripped the arms of her chair and stared out across the room as though piloting some unique and esoteric craft. 'I like it.'

I sipped my tea.

'It's because I was born under Uranus,' Beth said.

She began to reminisce about the years after the war, when Uncle Eric would invite her and Wendy to Dosthill Hall for a holiday. Dosthill was a Georgian mansion that stood on the banks of the River Tame, near Tamworth. Once the residence of Conservative prime minister and founder of the modern police force, Sir Robert Peel, it had a grass tennis court, a walled vegetable garden, and an ornamental lake with an island in the middle. The drive was sprinkled with pink marble chips from Italy. Eric had rented the place since the 1920s, and lived there with his older brother, Reg, and a gardener by the name of Shakespeare. In the family it was known as 'Dirty Dosthill' because no one ever did the dusting. By the fifties, most of the east wing had fallen into disrepair; chunks of ceiling plaster lay on the bare wooden floors, and the walls were mottled with damp. Beth recalled how she and Wendy would travel up by train.

'Wendy was very motherly. She organized the food. We had omelettes made with dried egg and water. They were horrible, leathery things, but we *loved* them. We used to eat ravenously, like wolves. Wendy would call out, Come on, Pansy. She always called me Pansy. I was slower than her.'

At Dosthill, they slept in the same room, she said, and they saw the ghost. I had heard the house was haunted, but had never seen the ghost myself. I asked what it looked like. It was a woman in a poke bonnet, Beth said, and a green silk dress down to the ground. The woman glided clockwise round the room; she didn't appear to have any feet. When she approached their beds, they froze.

'Do you mean the temperature dropped?' I said.

'Oh, it dropped *terribly*,' Beth said. 'And I said to Wendy after a while, Has she g-g-gone yet, Wendy? Do you think you could light the gas fire?'

While I was still laughing at the stutter, Beth jumped forwards in time. Prompted by her memory of the ghost, perhaps, she began to describe the day of Wendy's funeral. She had taken the train with Joe, she said. He had been in St Andrew's a few years before, receiving insulin shot treatment, and she thought it had 'sent him funny'.

'From London to Eastbourne, he never stopped talking. That was something mentally wrong. The train was going der-der-der-*der*, der-der-der-*der*, and Joe was talking all the time, and I nearly said, Shut *up*, Joe, for goodness sake.'

'Do you think he was upset by Wendy's death?'

'Not exactly, no. He said Wendy was where she always wanted to be – with God.' Beth drew a hand across her forehead, as if to wipe away perspiration. 'I don't think they saw much of each other.'

She told me that on the day of the funeral I was sent to play with a friend. People felt it would be good for me, better than moping around. Robin was ill. He stayed in Wendy's bed, next to my father's. He was very pale, but smiling – wanly, she thought the word was. I asked about Ralph. Beth told me she had walked into the dining-room and seen my father, with Ralph beside him, standing on a chair. My father had his arm round Ralph, and they were looking through the window at all the wreaths laid on the drive. The image was so poignant that I didn't know what to say, but Beth spoke for me:

'Poor little fellow.'

'But he didn't go to the funeral?' I said.

'None of you did. I went, though. They had "All Things Bright and Beautiful", and I could hear Wendy singing that. You know, she loved it. Lovely nature hymn. Little tiny wings and all that kind of thing. And then she was buried up at the cemetery.' Beth lifted her mug, which shook dramatically, and sucked some tea up through the straw. 'Later on,' she said, 'your father asked me if I'd mind him being buried with Wendy – he had remarried, you see – and I said, I don't mind at all, Rod, because Wendy was very much in love with you. I'd never seen Wendy so happy. When she got engaged, she was leaping round the room stark naked at Dosthill, and her boobs were going up and down, they were so large, she was giggling her head off, and I asked if I could touch one of them, because I had ping-pong balls, and she said, *No*, Pansy. We were listening to "Don't Let the Stars Get in Your Eyes". She had brought the record up to the Hall, and she was leaping around to it –'

'Do you know who sang it?'

'No. But it was very catchy. And I said, Oh, go on, let me touch one – I wanted to know what it was like, having big ones – and Wendy said, All right then, but only for a second. So I poked one on the side, and it was like warm rubber, and Wendy said, That's enough now. But we had a very personal relationship – not lesbian . . .' Using both hands, Beth placed her mug of tea on the pile of paper to her right. 'We got on really well. She was great fun.'

'What was her voice like?' I asked.

'I thought it was –' Beth hesitated – 'childish, rather. Young. Very young and innocent.'

'Even when she was in her twenties?'

'Yes. But I liked it. She was very, very sincere as a person, and you could see and hear that sincerity.'

'People often talk about her high spirits . . .'

'Yes. Full of energy. Heart people are. She was always wanting us to go off and do something. I couldn't keep up with her.' Beth lifted her mug, which wobbled precariously. 'She was strong – physically. She could bend everywhere. She didn't have any injuries.'

'Did she have any boyfriends before Dad?'

'That was very interesting. I felt far more worldly in that way – more earthy.'

I remembered Beth telling me how she had driven over to the mill once, for a shareholders' meeting, and how the company accountant had pinned her up against the wall of his office. Oh, he was *mad* on women, she had told me. His kisses had tasted of cigarettes, apparently, and his moustache had tickled her nose, making her want to sneeze. Afterwards, he pressed a ten-pound note into her hand, for petrol. Take it, Beth, he'd said. It's your money, after all.

But Beth was talking about my mother. 'I think it was her religion that held her back from going out with too many,' she said, 'and I don't think she'd permit hardly anything, if you know what I mean. She was a believer, through reading the bible and going to church such a lot.'

'She might have gone on dates, then,' I said, 'but nothing would have happened.'

'No. She was very strict. She enjoyed it, but in an innocent way.'

'That fits in with what you said about her voice.'

Beth nodded firmly. 'Yes.'

'So it's possible,' I said slowly, 'that my father was the only man she was ever with?'

'Oh yes, I'm sure.' And then, almost in the same breath, 'She told me that she went on top. Because Rod couldn't. He wasn't well enough. Got exhausted.'

Earlier, I had been speculating on the workload Wendy must have had, with a disabled husband, three young children, and no help in the house, and Beth had exclaimed, 'She was a *slave*.' The vehemence had startled me. Once, Beth said, while staying with my parents, she had followed Wendy out to the scullery after lunch to see if there was anything she could do. Rod had already gone upstairs to lie down. She helped clear the table and wash up, then watched as Wendy poured some milk into a pan. It was for Rod, Wendy told her. He always had hot milk before his rest. Since Wendy had been on her feet all day, Beth offered to take the milk upstairs for her. No, no, Wendy said. Rod liked her to do it. She did everything for him, Beth had told me. She had four children, really.

I asked Beth if Wendy had ever seemed tired.

'Within the last year of her life,' Beth said. 'The last few months. She came up to Dosthill, and I noticed that her facial colour had changed.'

'How?'

'It was more transparent – almost blue. And she seemed very tired then. Rod – your father – was talking to me in the red room, and after so long Wendy said, That's enough, Pansy. But it was because *she* was tired . . .'

I shifted on the green chaise longue. The deep carpet of paper – clothing catalogues, holiday brochures, order forms for book clubs – rustled beneath my shoes. Over the years, various people had voiced theories about my mother's premature death, the most common being that the contraceptive pill had killed her – instances of blood-clotting were reported in medical journals as early as 1968 – but perhaps she had simply taken on more than she could manage and had worn herself out.

'She really worshipped you,' Beth said suddenly.

'Did she? I mean, how do you know?'

'Oh, you could see it. In her face. And the way she hugged you! I remember, once, it was so cold, and she was in a sweater, hugging you as tightly as she could . . .'

It ought not to have been a surprise to hear that my mother loved me – I was the firstborn, and there were plenty of photos of us together – but I had always had to take that love on trust. I'd had to make up what she felt – to *imagine* how strong it must have been. I'd never actually *known*. Though I was grateful for Beth's words, there was also a part of me that refused to believe her, and wanted proof.

'Are you warm enough?' Beth asked.

'I think so,' I said.

'Do you need a wee?'

I spluttered. 'No –'

'You mustn't be shy.'

'I'm not, Beth. Really. I just don't have to go that often.'

'Shall we make our meal, then?'

Woken at eight the next morning by the steady crash of rain on the trees outside my window, I stepped on to the landing. Beth's door was wide open. She was lying on her side, facing away from me, the blankets heaped around her neck. I stood in her bedroom doorway, and thought of all the other mornings, her asleep and no one to watch over her, no one there. Years ago, she had told me she'd seen policemen in her garden. They took up positions in the bushes, or sometimes they sat about under the fig tree. They were concerned for her security, but she was convinced they fancied her as well. They had binoculars, she said. She would leave newspapers and magazines out for them, and in the summer she bought ice-creams. *They never ate them, of course.* I thought of how she had lost her father to cirrhosis of the liver when she was three. Her mother, Margaret, still only twenty-seven, and beautiful, was an alcoholic too. She drifted from man to man, and Beth and her sister, Connie, were constantly being shunted off to various relations. As a teenager, Beth had even stayed with my grandparents in Rokkosan. *Jim was the closest thing I had to a father*, she had said. *Uncle Eric would never put an arm round you.* After the war, when she was studying art at the Royal College, she moved back in with her mother, who lived near Kew Gardens, but there was never any food in the house, and the drunks Margaret brought home from the pub would frighten her. Once, a second-hand car salesman with glassy eyes had chased her round the sofa. *Mother was being naughty.* Connie would often have to call the police. Beth was so hungry she couldn't sleep. *Actually, I was very near suicide.* She was saved by her dog, Blackie, and their long walks in the dark along the south bank of the Thames. Connie had a job in a department store, and she bought tinned peaches and salmon, which she hoarded in her bedroom. Connie ate in secret. Margaret drank. *When you starve*, Beth had told me, *everyone sounds miles away*. She'd ended up at Dosthill, as she so often had as a child. She lived with her two uncles, Eric and Reg, for almost twenty years, and then, when Eric died in 1972, she used her legacy to move to Gloucestershire. She had been here ever since. The previous night, before going up to bed, I had walked into the kitchen and opened the fridge. Six as yet unopened two-pint cartons of milk stood shoulder to shoulder on the inside of the door, a wall against privation, against the past. I stepped back on to the landing, leaving my auntie to sleep on.

Later, over breakfast, I brought up the subject of religion. I was thinking of what Uncle Joe had said on the way to my mother's funeral. *She's where she always wanted to be – with God.* Beth talked about how devout my mother was, and how she used to kneel by her bed at night and pray, even after she was married. Neither of us was sure where this religious conviction had come from.

'I mean, it was a *good* thing,' Beth said, 'because she was a real Christian, but it worried me. Whether she knew – whether she had an idea –'

'That she might die, you mean?'

'She said to me once, I would hate to grow old. She had seen how Pim went, very old and wrinkly, with needle-holes all over her. I think she had a vision of ending up like that . . .'

And her wish had been granted: she had died young, even before her own mother.

The morning darkened. The rubbish in Beth's living-room, which had looked white the day before, had taken on a greenish tinge. I carried our breakfast plates out to the kitchen and started washing up. Beth stood next to me and dried.

'Uncle Reg had religious mania,' she said.

I remembered Reg from visits to Dosthill when I was a boy. He had small, furtive eyes and a bristling moustache, and his ears stuck out sideways, as if keen to gather sound. His voice had the pinched, nasal rasp of a two-stroke motorbike. Beth could imitate it perfectly. There was the time he led me off into the village without telling my parents, and for an hour they were panic-stricken, convinced that I had been abducted. Reg's room was at the top of the house. His clothes hung all round the walls. Beth had told me that mice lived in his suits. I asked if they were pet mice. Oh no, she said. Wild. Reg liked to stuff his pockets with biscuits, she said, and the crumbs attracted them. She also told me that a pigeon nested in the trilby that he kept on top of the wardrobe. Reg was a great believer in callisthenics. Once, Connie and a boyfriend were walking up the drive when they glimpsed a flash of white over by the lake. Naked from the waist down, Reg was lying on the grass with his legs in the air, doing his cycling exercises. Connie and her boyfriend burst into the kitchen, helpless with laughter. There was talk of a caterpillar and two peas. At the age of eighty-four, while winding the grandfather clock by the front door, Reg's foot became entangled in the chains that worked the pendulum. He tried to extricate himself, but pulled too hard. Ironing in her room, Beth heard the crash. She hurried downstairs and found Reg on his back, under the clock, with just his little coconut head and one boot sticking out. He died two months later, on a Sunday, after eating a bowl of soup. That was one story. But I had also been told that Reg had fallen asleep in front of the big gas fire in the dining-room, and that when he woke, his socks were in flames, and that the shock had killed him. All that could reliably be said about Reg's death, it seemed, was that some kind of domestic object had been involved.

'He could preach so beautifully,' Beth was saying. 'I remember calling Joe. Come and sit on the stairs, I said. I want you to listen to Uncle Reg. He's preaching in his bedroom. Honestly, it was so moving. He could use his voice like a really good actor. And Joe said afterwards that it was one of the best sermons he had ever heard.'

'Reg never married, did he?' I said.

'No.'

'Did he ever –'

'Have sex?'

I nodded.

'No, he didn't,' Beth said. 'He kissed a woman once, on the pier at Llandudno, and he said afterwards, That's enough, that's all. And that was as much as he ever did.'

'It might have been against his religion,' I said.

'Yes.'

I ran more hot water into the sink.

'Uncle Reg burned sprouts regularly,' Beth said. 'He would go upstairs to pray while they were cooking, and I'd think, What's that terrible *stink* coming in under the door? I'd go down into the main kitchen, and there were black balls that used to be sprouts all burnt in the bottom of the saucepan, and the heat still on. Reg would come galloping down because he would suddenly remember, and I'd say, Too late, Uncle.' She chuckled affectionately. 'Eric used to spend hours scouring Reg's pans.'

We fell quiet. There was just the clink of cutlery and plates in the sink, and the splash of rain on the Japanese mountain ash outside the window.

'Ralph's religious, isn't he?' Beth said.

'I don't know,' I said. 'I haven't seen him for years.'

'Haven't you?'

'Most of the time I forget he even exists. But then something happens, and I remember.' Once, in 1992, while I was living in London, one of Ralph's credit card statements was sent to me by mistake, and I couldn't help noticing that his credit limit was six times as big as mine. He seemed to be doing a lot better than I was. 'Frank's in touch with him,' I said. 'I could ask Frank, I suppose.'

Beth turned her strangely kind yet startled gaze on me. 'You should.'

I pulled the plug and let the water drain out of the sink. 'I think we've finished.'

'You *are* good,' Beth said.

I grinned. 'Not always.'

It was still raining when the time came for me to leave, but Beth wanted to see me off. She put on a fawn raincoat, which she had got from Save the Children. Ten pounds it had cost, she told me. One of her best buys ever. As I pulled away, I opened my window and looked out. Beth was standing by the garage in the downpour, bareheaded, waving.

That morning, as we ate our eggs and bacon, I had promised to visit her again soon.

'You'd better,' she said.

A Helicopter Crash

One morning in late March, I push the kitchen door open. Ralph and Vivian are sitting at the table. Shoulders hunched, head tilted at an angle, Ralph seems utterly absorbed by what Vivian is telling him. I fetch a bowl of Weetabix and sit down with my back to the window.

'You're going to die when you're forty-five,' Vivian says in a soft voice.

'Oh.' Ralph looks crestfallen, but his eyes don't leave her face. His whole body slants in her direction.

She reaches out and puts a hand on his. 'Sorry.'

She appears taken aback by what she has just said, as if it came from somewhere outside her – as if, like a medium, she is merely channelling the information, and isn't capable of exercising discretion or control.

My first instinct is to spring to Ralph's defence, but I quickly notice that he doesn't need defending. If anything, in fact, Vivian's prediction of his death has drawn them closer. Ralph has wrapped his hand round hers, and they are looking deep into each other's eyes. Are they always so brutally honest with each other? If that is the case, perhaps

I have been given an insight into the strength of the bond that exists between them. Ralph can handle any news, no matter how bad, provided he hears it from Vivian. And vice versa, presumably.

'So when am I going to die, then?' I ask.

Vivian turns to me and takes a long pull on her cigarette. Her eyes are ringed with black kohl, and her dark hair falls straight past her shoulders, making her face seem narrower than it is. She considers me for perhaps ten seconds.

'When you're fifty-eight,' she says.

'Great,' I say. 'Thanks for that.'

I glance at Ralph, and we exchange a rueful smile. If what Vivian is telling us is true, we are both already halfway through our lives.

At that moment, the door creaks open and Robin moves slowly into the kitchen, his big arms dangling. A deep tramline runs diagonally across the left side of his forehead. The jug of water doesn't appear to have worked this morning.

'What's going on?' he says.

I mention Vivian's predictions. He immediately wants to know how long he's got.

Vivian doesn't even bother turning round. 'Seventy-two,' she says.

For some reason, we all burst out laughing – all of us except Vivian, that is. She seems distracted, even absent, as though operating on a different level altogether, and I suddenly remember how Dad would refer to her as 'Svengali'. He claimed Ralph altered when he went to university – beyond all recognition, he would say – and he thought Vivian was the cause. The way he talked, you would think Ralph had been brainwashed, but now I'm sharing a house with Ralph and Vivian, I'm not convinced he was right. I think Ralph might have engineered the change himself. As soon as he left home, he was on the look-out for somebody to be with, somebody who would stay with him for ever, and the moment he met Vivian he knew she was the one. He couldn't wait to cast off the person he had been – that almost pitifully affectionate little boy who became attached to every au pair Dad employed and was then repeatedly abandoned.

He had to make sure that never happened again.

He had to make quite sure.

The following weekend, Robin and I have our first big fire, disposing of all the rubbish that the dustmen have refused to deal with. We feed the blaze with a tar-papered rabbit hutch, two rolls of carpet, and a box of toys that contains, among other things, a leprechaun, a plastic Rupert Bear, and several knitted gonks. The flames leap so high they char the branches of a nearby apple tree, and we worry briefly for the safety of the fence.

Later, we are down by the house, ransacking the main glasshouse for more items that might be flammable, when Robin happens to glance over his shoulder.

'Oh dear,' he says.

A column of oily smoke is rising from behind the hedge.

'It's the carpet,' I tell him. 'It's got a rubber underlay.'

'The neighbours aren't going to like it.'

'No. Probably not.'

Robin watches as the blue sky blackens. 'It looks like a helicopter's crashed,' he says.

When we have dealt with the contents of the glasshouse, I suggest the pink wardrobe, which I have no use for.

Robin's eyes light up. In my room, we lower the wardrobe on to its side, take one end each, and manhandle it out of the house.

'Now this,' Robin says, 'is *really* going to burn.'

He leads the way up the garden, his left arm underneath the wardrobe, his right arm hooked over the top. When he reaches the fire, he pauses. Since he seems to be about to heave the wardrobe into the middle of the fire, I quickly hoist my end and shove it hard towards him. He lets out a cry and doubles over, clutching his armpit. The wardrobe crashes to the ground.

'Shit,' he says. 'Fuck.'

Still hunched over, he gingerly lifts his shirt. A few dark drops land in the hot ash at the fringes of the fire. There is the pungent, medieval smell of burning blood.

'Sorry,' I say. 'I thought you were lifting it.'

'It slipped. I was adjusting it – fuck, this hurts.'

'Let me look.'

'Bastard piece of furniture.' Robin aims a savage kick at the wardrobe.

I peer at the wound. A splinter almost a foot long has pierced the skin under his right arm.

'At least it missed the artery,' I say.

'*Artery?* I could have *died*.'

'No, you couldn't.'

'Why not?'

'You're going to live to seventy-two, remember?'

'Vivian,' he snorts. 'What does she know?'

The cut needs stitches, though, and as I drive Robin to the hospital I think of the time he climbed on to the top of a five-bar gate at Uncle Roland's house when he was three. For a joke, I threw a picnic blanket over him. He looked, for a few moments, like someone pretending to be a ghost, then he lost his balance and toppled head first on to the concrete below. A sheet of blood slid down his face; his forehead began to swell. Suddenly I was alone on the drive, but I could hear his screaming coming from inside the house. It went on for longer than I thought possible. I wasn't sure how to look at anyone, or what to say, and I wasn't sure what I would see in their eyes when they looked at me.

In the car, I turn to Robin and apologize again. He tries to smile, but a wince appears instead.

'That's a nasty cut,' the doctor says in Casualty.

'A wardrobe did it,' Robin says.

Possibly because of her height – she is almost five eleven – Hanne tends to double over when amused or entertained, her knee bent, one foot lifting off the ground, and this is what she does when she emerges from Arrivals and sees me waiting at the barrier. Not for the first time, she reminds me, incongruously, of old-time comedians, the kind who slap their thighs after telling a joke. We kiss, then I stand back and admire the metallic silver suitcase she has brought with her.

'Yes,' she says. 'It's for you.'

Back at the house on Summerdown Road, she hands me the keys. I unfasten the locks and lift the lid. Inside, washed and folded, are all the clothes I left in West Berlin. There is my fifties' tropical-print shirt, the one with the label that says *Reminiscence,* and there are my black trousers, which I tore when I climbed into an abandoned S-bahn station in December. My first thought, which is quite involuntary, takes me by surprise: *She knows I'm not coming back.*

'I was thinking you will need your clothes,' she tells me simply. 'I was ironing them.'

'Hanne, that's so kind.'

'Yes –' and she is smiling now – 'I did it.'

I look at the neat piles of clothes and think of Leni, the daughter Hanne and I sometimes imagine we might have. The name, which rhymes with 'rainy', comes from Heinrich Böll's novel, *Group Portrait with Lady*, but whereas Böll's Leni is a well-preserved blonde of forty-eight, I see ours as a long-legged six-year-old with wavy light brown hair. In 1978 I went out with a Welsh girl who got pregnant. She didn't feel we should have the baby, and I agreed with her. We had only been together for a few months. We didn't know what the future held. We were still so young. Leni has never existed except as an idea, yet somehow she has always seemed more real to me than the child who was conceived and then aborted, the child who was never named. As I stare down into the suitcase, though, I see the likelihood of Leni's existence evaporate, silently but irrevocably, like a soap bubble exploding. Everything is disappearing, even things that never had the time to materialize. I feel such a keen sense of loss that I have to turn away. I don't want Hanne to ask me what is wrong.

I don't want to have to explain.

During Hanne's week in Eastbourne, Bill and Jenny Martin invite us over for a drink. When we leave our house one Friday evening at a quarter to seven, Ralph and Vivian join us. Vivian seems to be getting on with Hanne, and this one simple fact has been enough to turn us back into a group. It's dark out. The wind makes the trees roar, and the air smells earthy yet metallic, like the sharp end of a spade.

'Who are the Martins?' Hanne wonders as we cross the road.

'They're good people,' I say. 'They're friends.'

'Bill's in eggs,' Robin says.

Hanne looks puzzled.

I explain that Bill works for a company of egg brokers. If anyone ever asks him what he does, he always says the same thing: *I'm in eggs*.

'He has chickens?' Hanne says.

We're still laughing when one of the Martins' daughters, Belinda, answers the door.

'You lot are in a good mood,' she says drily.

We follow her into the front room, which is so much more comfortable than ours. Armchairs, a sofa. Lamps with shades in warm colours like butterscotch and terracotta. Bill turns from the fireplace. His black hair is neatly parted, and he is wearing a dark blue blazer and grey trousers. As always, he seems effortlessly genial and debonair.

'Nice to see you, Rupert. Gin-and-tonic?'

'I'm on the wagon, I'm afraid.'

To keep him from probing any further, I introduce him to Hanne. When he discovers that she is German, he is curious to know how we met. It happened the previous summer, I tell him, in Positano. I walked into a restaurant where Hanne and a girlfriend of hers were having dinner. I was sitting two tables away, but we kept catching each other's eye. When my first course arrived, I held up a spear of asparagus to show her what I had ordered. It promptly wilted in my hand. Neither of us could keep a straight face after that. Later, Hanne's friend invited me to join them at their table.

'It sort of went from there,' I say.

'I bet it did,' Bill says.

Jenny appears in the living-room doorway. She doesn't suppose anyone has made *her* a drink. As Bill reaches for the gin, she turns to Robin. 'We heard you the other night.'

On the night Hanne arrived, I persuaded Robin to get out his twelve-string guitar and sing. With hindsight, he thinks he might have got a bit carried away.

'We thought it was splendid,' Jenny says.

Robin grins. 'I can't imagine anyone else round here saying that.'

'Well, they're a bunch of fucking killjoys, aren't they?'

That's Jenny all over: generous but forthright, and with a wonderfully deadpan delivery. Despite Bill's suave demeanour, she seems older than him somehow, more worldly-wise – though I have the feeling this is a quality she has always had, even as a child.

Bill mentions a woman on Old Camp Road whose garden stands at right angles to ours. She has an outdoor swimming-pool, he says. Do we know her, by any chance? We shake our heads. She's not very happy, he goes on. Apparently, someone in the vicinity's been having fires. Flames in excess of twenty feet high have been reported. Little flakes of hot ash have floated on to the woman's property, burning holes in the tarpaulin that covers her pool.

'The thing is,' Robin says, 'a helicopter crashed in our back garden.'

'I see.' Bill calmly finishes his drink. 'Well, that explains the little flakes of ash.'

The woman knocked on his door, he tells us, wanting him to sign a petition in favour of banning fires.

'And did you?' Robin asks.

'Certainly not,' Bill says. 'I don't approve of petitions.'

Later, the conversation turns to food.

'What are you eating?' Jenny asks. '*Are* you eating?'

'Curry mostly,' Robin says.

'And Weetabix,' I say.

I tell Jenny that we have become addicted to buying in bulk. We do all our shopping in Macro, a wholesale place behind the station. Jenny says she's heard of it.

'Everything's much bigger than in real life,' Robin says.

'The milk comes in gallons,' I say.

'You get about two thousand tea bags, all in the same box,' Robin says.

I'm nodding. 'It's like they invented it for giants.'

Jenny shakes her head in despair.

Over by the fireplace, Hanne is talking about her job in the rehab unit – I hear the words 'Ernst' and 'bastard' – and Bill puts a hand on her forearm to show her that he sympathizes.

'I think Bill was rather taken with you,' I tell Hanne as we walk back over the road.

'What is taken?'

'He liked you.'

'Yes,' she says. 'He is a nice man. And she.'

No sex, the doctor told me, peering at me sternly, not until I have completed my course of antibiotics, but I am sharing a single bed with Hanne, and it's proving something of a torture. On our fourth night, as we lie side by side in the half-dark, Hanne asks if I'm awake. I say I am.

'Maybe tomorrow,' she says, 'we can try with coats . . .'

'Coats?' I seem to glimpse Dad's sheepskin hanging on a hook by the front door.

'Yes. Coats.'

I watch as her eyes travel down the bed, then up again. 'Oh, *coats*.' I start laughing.

The following day, I drive down to Boots the chemist. As I approach the display of condoms, it's all I can do not to pretend to be German. 'Please,' I very nearly say, in an accent resembling Hanne's, 'but do you have some coats?'

Not long after Hanne leaves, Dan invites me to come and stay. Dan used to be my art director, but he is now running the creative department of an agency in Newcastle, and he has bought a house outside the city, in a place called Stanley. I can have a room of my own to work in, he says. I can write all day if I want. No one will disturb me.

One April morning, Jenny Martin gives me a lift to the bus station. She asks after Hanne, as I suspected she might, and I remember Bill taking me aside on the night we went round for drinks. *I'd hold on to her if I were you.*

On the bus, I start a letter to Hanne. I want her to know what the Martins have been saying – it will cheer her up – but as I put pen to paper I am aware that other people's opinions will have little bearing on what happens between us. In the photos Robin took during Hanne's stay, we look playful and disingenuous, and there is nothing to suggest that our relationship is foundering, yet whenever I speak to her on the phone, or write to her, I seem unable to make any promises. All I feel sure of is my own uncertainty. And then I think of Tina by the fir tree in her black sweater, Tina with her troubled eyes and shoulder-length blonde hair . . .

The coach turns along the promenade. It's early, not even nine o'clock, and the light has a rare, scoured clarity. Low

tide, rock pools. People throwing balls for dogs. The sea
sprawls in the distance, tough and faintly rumpled, like a
bolt of dark blue leather. I used Hanne's time in Eastbourne
as an excuse to visit places I hadn't visited in years –
Michelham Priory, the Long Man of Wilmington, Ashdown
Forest. I wanted her to realize how significant they were,
and how precious – this was, after all, the map of my childhood – but I was also showing her what I'd grown out of,
and what I was now being forced, once again, to experience. It was all so familiar to me, so deeply ingrained, that
I found it hard to imagine what it must be like to be seeing
it for the first time. We walked the length of the seafront,
passing the white hotels, the bandstand, the Carpet
Gardens with their elaborate, geometric beds of flowers. I
took pictures of her on the pier, storm clouds stacked
behind her as she leaned against the railings. She wore a
pale green top and brown leather trousers, and her lipstick
was a glossy burgundy, like fallen rhododendron petals.
She thought it was a nice town, she said as I put my camera
away. It was *bürgerlich*. The word had become something
of a joke between us: Hanne claimed I disapproved of her
for being too interested in material things – for being too
bürgerlich. 'Yes –' and she glanced back along the promenade, chin tilting defiantly – 'I like it.' When she looked at
me again, she saw that I was laughing. 'You bastard.' She
aimed a punch at my left shoulder. 'Why are you laughing?'
But she was laughing too.

When I arrive in Newcastle, Dan picks me up in a silver
Ford. As we drive out of the city, over one of its many
bridges, we reminisce about my leaving party in 1982, and
how Dan wheeled me out of the building in the

supermarket trolley I'd been using instead of a chair, and how, later that evening, a six-foot-seven Irish copywriter tried to join me in the trolley, and it capsized, and I woke up the next morning with bruises all down the left side of my body.

In half an hour, we are pulling up outside Dan's new house in Stanley. With its high ceilings and its tiled hall, it ought to belong to someone middle-aged and respectable – a pillar of the community – but Dan is even younger than I am. Downstairs is a wood-panelled library with a full-size snooker table. Upstairs is a bathroom with an antique claw-foot bath. He has a sixties' Land Rover. He has two Dobermanns. I tell him I'm impressed, which is true, but my initial reaction is one of lightness: compared to Dan, I have so little. At the same time, I am being confronted by the kind of life that I have turned my back on. I don't feel envious so much as left behind, and a sense of panic stirs in me, faint but determined scratchings, like rain on a window.

Dan's wife, Brenda, says I can work in the room above the kitchen, and I start the following day, using a machine Dan has borrowed from his agency. I am writing about an eccentric village police force, and my sentences have been infiltrated by a humour that is both anarchic and surreal. I find this surprising at first, but then I remember the salacious constables who lurk in the bushes at the bottom of my auntie's garden with their dog-eared copies of the *Sun* and their binoculars. Once, at lunchtime, Brenda says she heard me chuckling as she ironed in the next room – *laughing at your own jokes*, as she puts it. But the book is beginning to thicken, take on a form, like beaten cream.

It's dark by the time Dan comes home, and we walk the dogs on the playing fields below the house. Most evenings, a raw wind is blowing, and the air smells of mud and coal and roots, as if it has more to do with the ground than the sky. Stanley has a long history as a mining town, Dan tells me, though many of the collieries have been closed down. Thatcher, I say. He nods grimly. We watch the dogs as they tear over the grass in exaggerated curves and loops, stopping to sniff at molehills or cock their legs against a goalpost. Dan says he's happy to have moved back up north. He sounds a little as though he's trying to convince himself: if he repeats the words often enough, they will end up being true. He asks what I will do next. Am I going back to Germany? I tell him I don't know. I want to write, but I can do that anywhere. My life is the opposite of his: shapeless as water, it can flow in any one of a hundred different directions.

'Has it been difficult?' he asks.

He is referring to Dad's death, a subject we have hardly mentioned.

'Really difficult,' I say. 'But the good side of it is I'm free – and there will be some money . . .'

Dan says I should come and live in Stanley. My resources will go much further. The house, the cars, the wine – he couldn't afford this quality of life down south.

I stare off into the dark, damp sky.

'At least think about it,' he says. 'You could stay with us while you sort yourself out.'

I thank him, then point at the two dogs, who are racing across a football pitch. 'Look at them. They're going mad.'

Dan nods. 'It's their favourite time of day.'

I return from the north-east with a new version of my novel under way. Determined to keep going, I lift the cover off my precious Olympia portable, only to discover that the keys are all bunched up and bent out of shape, like so many crossed fingers. The entire mechanism is jammed. Two months have passed since I flew to England, and it's almost certainly too late to contact British Airways and demand compensation. How can I prove the damage happened in transit? Furious at myself for having trusted that stewardess, I carry the typewriter downstairs and hurl it on to the heap of scrap metal near the garage. With a mocking twang, it lands among the spokes of a buckled bicycle wheel. Luckily, I have a back-up. An old office Olympia, it is uglier, and far more cumbersome, but it will have to do. With Robin's help, I haul Dad's teaching table up to my bedroom and set it down in front of the window that overlooks the garden, then I place the Olympia on a folded towel so as to muffle the thumping of its keys.

I decide to work at night, partly for the romance of it – William Faulkner is supposed to have written one of my favourite books, *As I Lay Dying*, between the hours of midnight and four a.m. – and partly to avoid interruptions. Every evening I make sure that I am sitting at my table by eleven. Propped against the window is a window frame I found on Hydra in 1977, the wood painted a chalky, dusty pale blue, a colour you almost never see in England. It reminds me of the time I got up early and crossed the high spine of the island, a thin brown path twisting before me like a trail of gunpowder, the air seasoned with wild sage and tingling with goat bells. Just me under the sky, and no one else about. Then a view down into a rocky bay, and a sudden feeling of slippage, as if a vessel from the long-distant past might slide out of the mist that rested on the sea, as if, merely by walking, I had unravelled time. A kind of spell about that morning: nothing happened, yet everything seemed possible.

What I need to do more than anything, I realize, is to put in the hours. While in Berlin, I read Rainer Maria Rilke's *Letters on Cézanne*. 'It seems to me,' he wrote in a letter dated 24 June 1907, 'that the ultimate intuitions and insights will only approach one who lives in his work and remains there.' I love his use of the word 'approach': it's as if intuitions and insights are wild beasts that don't show themselves unless the writer, like a hunter, stays upwind and motionless. Writing is about patience, cunning. Stamina.

As I toil over my sentences, the house falls quiet behind me. Robin climbs the stairs with his jug of water and his latest book. He reads on into the small hours; if I go down to the kitchen to make coffee, there is often still a bar of light under his door. Sometimes the baby wakes. I hear Vivian and Ralph murmuring. Her voice, then his. A key grates in the lock, the door clicks open. Feet pad across the landing. There is a silence, followed by the throaty flushing of the lavatory. A gargle as the cistern starts to fill again. More footsteps, another click. The key turns back the other way. In the corner of my room the dark air stirs, then settles. My eyes lower to the sheet of paper in the typewriter.

Remain there.

At six, I switch my desk lamp off. The garden surfaces. I stand and stretch. The grass is grey, no detail visible as yet. Dew makes the garage roof tiles gleam.

Later, I lie back between the sheets. I hear a creak on the stairs, and then the scrape of a chair leg on the kitchen floor, and then I drift away.

The Sauce is Nice

At the end of 2005, I drove down to Uncle Frank and Auntie Miriam's with my wife, Kate, and my daughter, Evie. For the past twenty years, Frank had been the only member of our family Ralph had been prepared to deal with. I had called Frank recently and asked about my brother, as Beth had urged me to, and he had told me that he had spent a day with Ralph and Vivian before they left for China, and that he had taken some photos. China? I said. He's got a new job, Frank said, in Shanghai. I asked if he would show me the pictures. It had been so long since I'd seen Ralph; I didn't know what he looked like any more. Such a bloody shame, Frank said.

When we arrived at the house, Miriam put the kettle on and Frank dropped into a wicker chair in the corner of the kitchen. He was lamenting the fact that we hardly ever saw each other. He wished we didn't live so far away. I reminded him that, not so long ago, when Kate's father, Fred, was ill with cancer, we had been living just up the road, in Cheshire. We hadn't seen much of each other then either.

'I *know*, I *know*,' Frank cried, closing his eyes and waggling his head. 'I kept *meaning* to drive up, but there was always something – always *something* . . .'

I couldn't help smiling. Frank liked to portray himself as put upon, if not victimized; it was as though immensely powerful forces had singled him out for special treatment.

'I've just been so *busy*,' he said, 'with the mill.'

He would never not be busy, I thought. How old was he? Eighty-one? Eighty-two? Frank was the opposite of most people. Anxiety seemed to keep him going.

I watched as he put a hand on my daughter's head. 'Such a dear little thing,' he said.

We moved to the dining-room. A crimson cloth covered the oak table, and candles burned in matching silver candelabras. We were halfway through the twelve days of Christmas, and a tall tree filled the bay window, its coloured lights ablaze. Sitting opposite me, Frank was surveying his plate. His mouth had turned down at the corners.

Miriam gazed at him steadily. 'What is it, Frank?'

'You *know* I can't stand chicken.' With a kind of frantic desperation, Frank scraped the mustard sauce off the chicken breast, then speared it with his knife and dumped it back into the solid silver serving-dish.

Miriam looked at me. We both smiled.

'The sauce is nice,' Frank said after a while.

Towards the end of the meal, I mentioned the photos of Ralph. Frank let out a groan. They were upstairs, in his study. He didn't know where, though. It all needed sorting out.

I reminded him that he had promised to let me see them.

'Did I?' he said.

For a moment he remained quite motionless. Then, all

of a sudden, he pushed his chair back, hauled himself to his feet and hurried out of the room, elbows jabbing at the air. I heard him making for his study on the first floor. Thump-thump-thump. He seemed to stamp on each stair rather than simply tread on it.

He returned five minutes later, empty-handed, head tipped back in despair. 'I don't know, Rups. I *thought* I had them.'

'I know where they are,' Miriam said.

A wail from Frank. '*No*, poppet, you can't go up there, poking around. You'll mess everything up.'

My aunt and I exchanged a glance.

Off he went again, to have another look. Stomp-stomp-stomp. Back he came. Still nothing. While he was eating his pudding, Miriam slipped out of the room. She re-appeared with a rectangular packet. 'Here we are.'

'Is that them?' Frank said. '*God*.'

The packet contained half a dozen snaps of Ralph and his family. The sky was a deep, flawless blue – the blue of childhood skies, the blue of the past – and Ralph was wearing a white short-sleeved shirt and loose white trousers, exactly the sort of clothes he had worn during the summer of 1984. In three of the pictures he had a cigarette between his fingers.

'So he smokes,' I said.

'Oh yes.' Frank nodded enthusiastically. 'Like a chimney.'

Ralph's hair had been receding when I last saw him. Now he was almost completely bald. He was pale too. In our family we were all pale – as a boy, people were always asking me if I was ill – but Ralph's pallor was pronounced, extreme: he looked as though he had spent his entire life under fluorescent lights. In one of the photos he was hugging his youngest daughter, and I was surprised at how strong his forearms were. The baldness, the pallor, the muscularity – I found myself thinking, incongruously, of Jean Genet.

I showed the pictures to my wife, Kate. She didn't think Ralph looked very well. He looked, she thought, like somebody who hadn't got too long to live.

'That's a terrible thing to say,' I said.

She shrugged, then grinned mischievously. 'Well,' she said, 'you asked.'

I studied the photos again. There was Ralph with his arm round Vivian. There were Ralph's children, three of whom I had never seen. These were my nephews and nieces, and yet I didn't even know their names. Was that my fault? Should I have made more of an effort?

I hadn't set eyes on Ralph since 1984, but my last contact had been in 1987. Sonya had asked us to release some money from the trust we had set up for Rosie and Hal. As executors of Dad's will, we needed to approve the request and to sign the appropriate forms, but neither Robin nor I knew where Ralph lived. Frank thought Ralph worked for an Italian bank in the City. He didn't have a clue which one, though. I consulted the phone directory. There were about twenty-five banks with Italian names. I rang them, one after the other. When I reached bank number eight, the receptionist put me through, and I heard Ralph say his name. 'Ralph,' I said, 'it's Rupert.' His first words were, 'How did you get this number?' He seemed on the point of hanging up. Despite being utterly wrong-footed, I managed to persuade him to stay on the line. At the end of the call, however, he told me not to ring him again. If I wanted to make contact, I should do so in writing. Shocked by the formality – the *finality* – of what he was saying, I laughed. In writing. As if I were dealing with a lawyer. Over the years I had abided by his ruling – I hadn't called; I hadn't even written – but now, in my uncle's dining-room, it occurred to me that since there were two parties involved, Ralph and me, surely I had *some* say in the matter. I thought about what Kate had said when she saw the pictures. *He looks like someone who hasn't got too long to live.* With a jolt, I remembered Vivian giving him until he was forty-five. I did a rapid mental calculation: Ralph had celebrated his forty-fifth birthday in September, just over three months ago! I didn't take Vivian's prediction seriously, but all the same . . . It would be strange, wouldn't it, if we were to die without ever seeing each other again? It would be strange if I didn't at least make a stab at solving the mystery of what had come between us. I didn't think Ralph would reach out, though, not after all these years. I wasn't sure he would be capable, or even interested.

In which case it would be up to me.

Not What He Would Have Wanted

In the letter he wrote to accompany his will, Dad assumes we will be keeping the house in the family, and though Ralph has been considering the idea – it's a good place to bring up children, and he and Vivian are planning on having more – he doubts he will be able to borrow enough money to buy myself and Robin out. This leaves us with no option but to put the house on the market.

In the middle of May, we ring a firm of estate agents, requesting a valuation. The following day, I answer the door to a man in a suit whose hair is the colour of saw-dust, and I'm not sure I don't catch a faint whiff of teak or maple as he brushes past me into the hall. Methodically, he moves from room to room, almost all of which are private galleries for Dad's innumerable paintings, and I sense surprise, bewilderment, and even, just occasionally, a bright flash of alarm. I watch him peer up into the stairwell, its mint green wall dominated by several abstracts in the style of Jackson Pollock. 'Most unusually appointed,' he murmurs.

Once he has completed his inspection, he recommends

an asking price, which I discuss with Robin and Ralph that same evening. The next morning, we ring the estate agents and give them the go-ahead. Not long afterwards, a photograph of our house appears in the *Herald* with the words SOUGHT AFTER SUMMERDOWN ROAD beneath.

Within ten days, a local architect has offered the asking price, and the sale is agreed, with completion to take place on the thirteenth of September. At midday on that date the property must be empty, the man with the wooden hair informs us. If we fail to comply, we will be subject to financial penalties. Though this is the news I have been waiting for, I retreat to my bedroom and, sitting at my writing-table, stare out over the garden. The main obstacle to my leaving Eastbourne has been removed. In three months' time I will be free to go anywhere I want. Why, then, is my stomach turning over? Why do I feel as if I might be sick?

A breeze pushes past me, the smell of roses in full bloom and new-mown grass tempered by hints of ash and rubber from our most recent fire. I imagine my grandparents first viewing the property on a day like today. With its walls of grey pebble-dash and its steep slate roof, the house had never looked particularly inviting, and the diamond-paned windows in the front rooms only added to the air of melancholy, but all that would have been forgotten when James Gausden saw the cherry trees that lined the south side of the garden. The sight would have reminded him of the cherry blossom festival, one of the more significant events in the Japanese calendar. He might even have muttered the word under his breath. *Ohanami.*

'This is the place, Pim,' he would have said.

And Pim would have murmured, 'Yes.'

Her husband was not a man you disagreed with.

In photographs taken before the First World War, when he was still a bachelor, my grandfather often appears in a white suit and white shoes, with a cigarette between his fingers. He reminds me of certain film stars from the silent era – Ronald Coleman, or Douglas Fairbanks Junior. Whether seated at the dinner table in his club or lounging in some house of doubtful repute, he exudes a supreme sense of entitlement: he could do anything, have anything – including, as even a cursory reading of his diaries attests, the young women in kimonos who stand coyly in the background. I never met him – he died seven years before I was born – but something of his character can be glimpsed in an interview he gave to one of the national daily papers in 1920. 'When I first came to Japan,' the 'Lady Reporter' quotes him as saying, with a smile on his 'still rosy cheeks', 'you were a babe-at-arms, to be sure . . .'

James Gausden was employed in a managerial capacity by a succession of American oil companies. A passionate mountaineer, known among fellow members of the Alpine Club as 'the Mountain Goat', he is believed to have scaled every notable peak in Japan. He was a photographer too, his expeditions recorded in black and white at first, and then in a series of exquisite colour plates. He had arrived in Tokyo in 1900, aged twenty-one, and returned to England only once, when he was forty, to look for a wife. He found her in Eastbourne, at the annual tennis tournament in Devonshire Park. Her name was Winifred Tolson, though most people knew her as Pim, the nickname taken from a fish-and-chip shop called Pim's that she'd been mad about when she was growing up. James assumed she was in her twenties, and she was either too embarrassed or too ashamed to correct him, and they were married within a month, in a village church in Staffordshire. After the wedding, James left for Japan, travelling west this time, since there were mountains in the United States that he was eager to attempt. Some weeks later, Pim set off for the Far East on a P&O steamship to start her new life as a married woman. She had the first of her nervous breakdowns shortly afterwards, brought on by the certain knowledge that she would never see her father alive again.

The Gausdens lived in Tokyo to begin with, then moved to Kobe. Despite Pim's age, she had three children: Francis was born in 1923, Cedric in 1928, and Wendy in 1931. Pim would have been forty-six when she gave birth to my mother. When did Jim find out how old she was? I don't know. But he did. Frank once told me that his father 'was very cross about it'. 'Oh yes,' Frank went on, '*very* cross. Mummy was much older than she looked, you see. Not at *all* what he would have wanted.' Did Jim feel deceived, or cheated? Again, it's impossible to know. A marriage, children – this was what society expected, and he had kept his side of the bargain, yet I have the nagging suspicion that family life failed to engage him fully. Did he go on seeing the young Japanese women who were so readily available? I can't say. If he wrote diaries after 1920, I have never seen them. His passion for mountaineering didn't fade, though, nor did his interest in photography. When the Great Kanto earthquake hit the Tokyo area in September 1923, Jim hurried home from the office, not to check on the safety of his wife and new-born son – they were in the garden, part of the house having collapsed – but to pick up his precious Voigtländer. He spent hours in Yokohama that day, taking more than a hundred pictures of the devastation.

In 1934, with Jim's retirement looming and Japanese nationalism on the rise, the Gausdens were sent back to

England. According to Frank, his father was 'furious'; the way of life that he had loved was over. At first they lived in a Buckinghamshire village, near the Thames, then they moved to Eastbourne, the place where they had met. When Jim bought the house in Summerdown Road, he named it 'Rokkosan', after the mountain that overlooks Kobe, and that mysterious word was still on the front gate when I was a boy, though I never gave it too much thought. All the houses in our road had funny names. Arklow, Frimleigh. Buttevant.

In a large dark green album that dates from the late thirties or early forties, I find a photograph of Jim standing outside the main glasshouse, his right hand clamped on my mother's shoulder. Bald and portly, his eyes concealed behind a pair of wire-rimmed spectacles, he has an austere, draconian air. He might be the chief interrogator in a total-itarian state. He might even be a dictator. Had he not been posing with my mother, I'm not sure I would have realized that it was him; certainly there is no trace of the film-star looks. When I was in my teens, I remember Dad saying that he got a shock whenever he saw himself in the mirror. The passing of time makes us unrecognizable, even to our-selves; age is a kind of fancy dress that no one can take off.

The physical change in my grandfather is so pronounced that it is tempting to link it with his premature, enforced departure from Japan. I once asked Georgina, a close friend of my mother's, what it was like to visit the house on Summerdown Road during that time. She hardly ever saw Wendy's father, she said. He would be locked in his study, and would only venture out for meals. She spoke briefly of a cruel streak. *He used to hit them a bit.* Years later, she wondered whether he might have been struggling with depression.

A picture of Pim in the same album shows her on the back lawn in a pale shift dress and flat shoes. Her hair is white. This happened overnight, apparently, during the earthquake of 1923. With her thick waist and her square hands, she looks clumsy, almost mannish, and her smile, which reveals large, uneven teeth, has a precarious quality, like a plate balanced on a stick. Though she is giving the photographer – her husband, presumably – a passable impression of happiness, tears don't seem far away. According to Frank, his father had been so domineering that his death left a kind of vacuum. On her own suddenly, Pim became 'mentally poorly', 'sad and weeping', 'deranged'. I turn back to the photo. She must have known this would be their last home, but did she also suspect that it would be here, in this house, that her life would start to unravel?

I have always been drawn to my mother's side of the family, but now that I am back in the house, and back for the last time, I can feel the connection tightening, becoming almost visceral. My mother's parents lived here. My mother lived here too. So did my mother's brothers, Frank and Joe, and so, for a while, did her favourite cousin, Beth. They ate and slept in these small, awkwardly shaped rooms. They laughed and cried. Some lost their minds. Others died. Three generations have been superimposed, one on top of the other; there are times when the air feels crowded. In selling the house, we'll not only be disregarding my father's wishes. We'll be disposing of my mother's history, and our own.

I get up from the table. Leaving my room, I walk down the stairs and out through the front door. I pull it shut behind me. The rattle of the metal letter box, the solid shudder of the lock. A clock strikes two. When I think of my childhood in this house, it is always early afternoon, the part of the day when time seemed to slow down, to swirl and then disperse, like ink in water. I step away from the door, then come to a halt. I am standing in the place where I last heard – or thought I heard – my mother's voice.

She died playing tennis. She was about to serve. The courts where it happened, Manor Gardens, are located in Gildredge Park, only a few minutes' walk away.

The day after we accept the offer on the house, I decide to go on a pilgrimage. Turning left out of our front gate, I take the first right into Vicarage Road. The pavement tilts unevenly, its weathered bricks forced upwards by the roots of the elm trees that are planted at regular intervals on the south side of the street. On the north side the houses are clad in red scalloped tiles, and flint walls enclose the small front gardens. The windows are all blank. Most of the residents are old, and live alone.

I pass the vicarage, a vast, rambling place, its window frames and drainpipes painted yellow. Beyond the vicarage is Love Lane, an unpaved track that runs past the back of my mother's school. I move on along the road. The houses become fancier, with white clapboard gables. White wooden balconies cling to the upper storeys. It's so quiet and still that I can hear my own breathing. A cloud appearing from behind a clump of fir trees makes me jump.

I enter the park through a green metal gate. The world tightens around me. I have been here so many times, but not for years. My mind drifts back to 7 July 1964. A game of mixed doubles had been arranged. My mother set off up the road in her tennis clothes. White pleated skirt, white plimsolls. She would have been carrying her racket, its head zipped into a beige canvas cover. I don't know who partnered her, but I seem to recall that one of the players was a doctor. When she collapsed on court, her friends must have thought she had fainted. It was a hot day. I imagine the doctor hurdling the net, but she was dead before he reached her. Then what? Someone must have hurried to a phone and called an ambulance. The others would have stayed with the body. Did they cover her? Did a small crowd gather? Who told my father?

I see the courts off to my right. Pigeons scatter as I approach. Though summer has hardly started yet, the air smells bitter, autumnal. I cross the wet grass and hook my fingers through the wire mesh. Grey asphalt, neat white lines. The net sags between its posts. A high laurel hedge on two sides, leaves dark and glossy. I try to picture the scene, as if I am someone who just happened to be walking through the park that day . . .

A Tuesday morning in July. The air already warm, sharp edges to the shadows. Four friends in their thirties. The scuff and squeak of gym shoes, a grunt as a player stretches to smash a lob. A groan of despair. Then laughter. A woman with dark hair is about to serve. As the ball loops up into the air, she draws her racket back, hips swivelling, left knee bent. She lets out a cry, then crumples. A moment of stillness. Only the ball is moving, bouncing away across the court. A man drops his racket, leaps over the net. His partner has covered her mouth. Her hair is gold in the bright sunlight, and her shoulders hunch, as if she is expecting a deluge of cold water. Behind her, the laurel hedge looks black. The dark-haired woman is lying on the ground. The ball fetches up against the wire-mesh fence, irrelevant, forgotten . . .

Later, as I pass the pavilion with its ice-cream kiosk, I remember how I found my mother's racket once, by chance, in the box room. Dad must have hidden it, unable to bring himself to throw it away. The handle was bound with strips of dark-blue leather made darker still by sweat. Her sweat. I realized this was the last thing that she ever touched. I put my nose to the handle. Musty, ancient – utterly impersonal. Even the smell of her had faded.

I sit on a swing, pretending not to have noticed the sign that says CHILDREN UNDER 14 ONLY. It's term time, a week-day; there's hardly anyone about. I grip the metal chains. You can try your utmost to get back, you can do all the imagining you want, but you can't change the fact that you weren't there. I tuck my legs under the seat, then thrust them out in front of me. The sky tilts. My stomach lurches, and is left behind.

Horrible Trees

While in Eastbourne in 2007, I called in on Dr and Mrs Mynott, who had been friends of my parents in the fifties and early sixties. I had always known that Rosalind Mynott was one of the people who had been playing tennis with my mother when she died, but I had never spoken to her about it. Thinking the Mynotts might be able to bring me closer to the events of that day, I had phoned and asked if I could pay them a visit.

When I arrived, Dr Mynott showed me into the living-room. Rosalind was standing by a picture window, the muted colours of the garden behind her. She stuttered, just as she used to when I was a child, blinking rapidly if a word eluded her, and it was this more than anything that gave me the feeling that time had dissolved, and that we were all the same age as we had been when we last saw each other, and for a few uncanny seconds I was sure that if I looked down at myself I would see grey shorts, bare knees.

I took a seat by the window, and the doctor settled in a wing-backed chair across the room. Rosalind stepped into the kitchen to make tea. When she returned, I smiled up at her. Stopping in front of me, she reached down, took my face in both hands and kissed me on the forehead. Driving into Eastbourne that morning, I'd had an image of Rosalind as a brisk, no-nonsense woman, but this spontaneous gesture revealed a side of her that I had forgotten.

While she cut me a slice of cake, I filled her in on my behaviour following my mother's death. Auntie Miriam had told me that I had carried on almost as if nothing had happened, though sometimes I would run into the house and call out, 'Mummy?'

'I would forget, you see?'

Rosalind stared at the carpet, her eyes liquid, opaque.

I asked her what she remembered of my mother.

'Well, she was very, very pretty.' Rosalind lifted her cup, then lowered it again without drinking. 'She was always cheerful and enthusiastic and welcoming, whereas I think your father was inclined to be a bit dour, perhaps.'

I asked if they'd had many friends. Rosalind thought they had, but couldn't recall any of their names. When I tried to prompt her by suggesting that some of the socializing might have revolved around tennis, she started to describe the day my mother died. She talked quickly, her words eroding, incomplete, as if snatched from her mouth by a strong wind.

'I know there were eight of us – we were playing at Devonshire Park – there were *eight* – two lots of four – I was serving, and I'd turned round to get the balls – and I looked back, and Wendy had collapsed –'

'*You* were serving?'

She nodded. 'Yes.'

I had always imagined my mother was serving – it was

what I had been told, perhaps – but Rosalind had been there, on court. It wasn't a game of mixed doubles either; no men had been involved. Not a doctor, then. A doctor's wife. I didn't know what to ask next. The atmosphere in the room seemed troubled suddenly, and tense.

'So she collapsed,' I said slowly. 'What happened then?'

Dr Mynott remembered that his wife had called him at his practice, and that he had hurried round to the tennis courts. But by then, of course, it was already too late. 'These things happen just like that,' he said.

I spoke to Rosalind. 'Where did you say you were playing?'

'Devonshire Park,' she said.

'Are you sure?'

'Yes,' Dr Mynott said. 'I remember it quite clearly.'

Rosalind was nodding. 'I can picture it.'

I thought back to my pilgrimage of 1984. I had imagined my mother dying in Manor Gardens – I had brought the day of her death to life, and it had felt so real, so *authentic* – but now it turned out she hadn't died there at all. She had died somewhere else entirely. I smiled sadly down into my tea.

'I have no recollection of who else was playing,' Rosalind said. 'And of course we didn't play again. We were so completely shattered.'

With no other leads to follow, it looked as if Rosalind might be my only source, but when I pressed her for more memories of that day, she shook her head. She didn't think she had anything to add.

'She just collapsed.' Rosalind touched the cake crumbs on her plate with the tip of a finger. 'I think of her with a fringe, and her hair in a ponytail. Always cheerful and smiling and friendly – a ray of sunshine, really.'

'One of those people who make you feel better when you see them?'

Rosalind nodded. 'Eternally youthful – and that, of course, is how you remember her. Because she died as such a young woman.'

It was as though my mother's character was also her destiny. I remembered how her piety had worried Auntie Beth, and how Beth had suspected Wendy of knowing something no one else knew – not consciously, but in her blood, her bones. Her high spirits became more significant if they were set against a fast approaching darkness. In 2006, I opened a book by Imre Kertész and came across the following phrase: *that fragile gift bestowed for an uncertain time*. In just eight words, Kertész had captured what it was like to grow up in my family. I never had the feeling I would live for ever. Immortal? We're about as immortal as dandelion flowers. One breath of wind, and we're half gone. Another breath. That's it. All over. My mother's death taught me that the things I took for granted could be taken from me. The ground could open up; the sky could fall. Life was as flimsy as the model planes I used to buy, all balsa wood and rubber bands.

The doctor and his wife walked me to my car.

'Strange that she died in Devonshire Park,' I said. 'It's where her parents met.'

'Really?' the doctor said. 'We didn't know.'

As I drove away, I felt I was still lacking the one detail or fragment that would help me to see my mother's final moments – the real-life equivalent of the ball bouncing away across the court – and it was possible no one could supply it, though I couldn't shake the feeling that I might have learned more if I'd interviewed the Mynotts separately. It was only a few days later, though, when I was back home in Barcelona, that I realized what I would have to do.

I flew to England again in the spring of 2008, staying the night with Bill and Jenny Martin, who were now living in lush farming country a few miles north of Eastbourne. The following morning, I rose early and drove into town. I arrived at the Mynotts' house at a quarter to nine to find them both dressed to go out, and it was apparent from the doctor's opening remarks that he was fully intending to join us. On the phone I had asked if Rosalind could come to Devonshire Park with me and show me exactly where my mother died, but maybe the doctor and his wife were used to doing things together, and I decided it would be insensitive of me, or even rude, to attempt to come between them.

Since Rosalind had an appointment at ten, we took two cars. The doctor led the way, and I followed in my rented Astra, with Rosalind beside me. We had been driving for less than a minute when she turned to me and said, 'There's something I should tell you. The tennis courts aren't there any more. It's a car park now.'

I looked at her, not sure what to make of this.

'The grass courts are still there,' she explained, 'but not the hard courts we were playing on.'

We passed the Congress Theatre, where building work was going on, then turned into the car park Rosalind had just alluded to. Once parked, we joined Dr Mynott, who was standing some twenty yards away. I asked Rosalind whether she could identify the place where my mother had collapsed.

The doctor responded first. 'Well,' and he lifted an arm and pointed, 'where that puddle is, frankly.'

He laughed, and I laughed with him, but Rosalind was staring at the ground. She was moved by the thought of my mother's death, perhaps, and also by my floundering attempts to get closer to it. She seemed to feel a responsibility to me: if she couldn't remember enough, she would be failing me, letting me down.

I followed her into an empty parking space, and we came to a halt between a grey Renault and a white Iveco van. In front of us lay an area of tarmac, which was where the puddle was. Beyond were more cars, all with their backs to us, and then a high flint wall and a row of trees shifting in the wind.

'I had just served,' Rosalind said, 'and I turned round to get a ball. I was going to serve again, into the left-hand court this time. And Wendy was on the other side of the net – actually over there.' She pointed at a silver Saab. 'And I turned round, and she had fallen down . . . But I know the trees were there. So there was a green – a green background.'

'Do you remember how she fell?'

'I don't. I wish I could.' Rosalind stared straight ahead. 'She was just lying on the ground when I turned round. Everything else is blank. The horror – and fear . . .' Looking up at me, she laid a hand on my shoulder.

We were silent for a moment.

'I wonder what kind of trees they are,' I said.

'They're – they're – they're *horrible* trees.' She spoke with such vehemence that I had to laugh. 'They're holm oaks, and the leaves fall all year round.'

She took me through some other aspects of the place that hadn't changed. Sometimes it was hard to hear her voice above the drilling from the building site nearby.

'And the weather was lovely?' I said.

She nodded. 'A lovely sunny day – and that only added to the horror of it . . .'

'But you can't remember how she looked?'

'She was just – just lying there . . .' All of a sudden, Rosalind lowered her chin and drew her right arm up in such a way that it encircled her forehead. Watching carefully, I thought she was telling me that my mother had fallen forwards, that she had ended up face-down on the court. Rosalind's gesture had the sketchy, haunting quality of a re-enactment, but it also looked like a portrayal of sorrow, as though, in that moment, she was imitating one of the stone angels you find in graveyards, as though she herself was grieving. *We were so shattered. We didn't play again.* I put a hand on her arm. The drilling became still more persistent.

'I'm sorry about the noise,' she said. 'Do you want a moment of quiet here?'

'We'll go and sit in our car,' the doctor said.

When they had walked away, I stood between the Renault and the van. Marked in white, the parking spaces seemed an eerie echo of the tennis courts they had superseded – eerie and yet logical, since the one looked like a reworking or corruption of the other. I took a photo with my mobile phone, then moved towards the place where my mother had collapsed. Kneeling by the Saab's rear bumper, I reached out and touched the ground, and for a moment I thought I could feel her there, beneath my hand, she was lying in the position Rosalind had hinted at, face down, one arm circling her head, and I had my hand on her back, in the space between her shoulder blades, the cotton of her shirt against my palm, she was still warm, and a murmur came out of me, as if I were comforting her, or comforting us both. The wind swooped, then dropped. A man passed behind me, car keys jingling.

Later that day, on Terminus Road, I made a hard copy of the picture I had taken. Three cars seen from the back, some shallow puddles – a few white lines . . . The photo seemed oddly empty, without a focal point.

No, more than that: it looked tampered with. As though the subject of the original picture had been removed, and all that remained was a background. She had been here once, right here. It had happened here. But she was gone.

The Sticky Cherubs

Since I started writing at night, I have stopped drinking in the evenings, and I usually sleep until two in the afternoon. Feeling at a loose end, perhaps, Robin announces that he is off to Wales. While at art college in Newport, he became close to a family called the Atwoods. Jeremy, the husband, was one of his tutors. Robin also knows Jeremy's wife, Lynne, and their two daughters. He is going to stay at their house, he says. He isn't sure how long he'll be away.

After about a week, he calls with some news. He has bought two Rover 90s for £600. Two? I say. The second one's for spares, he explains. He wants me to come to Wales. Obviously he can't drive both cars back to Eastbourne by himself. He needs my help.

'But I'd have to stop working,' I say.

'Only for a day or two. You can carry on when you get back.'

I hesitate.

'Think of it as an adventure,' Robin says.

I catch a train the following day. Arriving in Newport

in the late afternoon, I ring the Atwoods' house from a phone box outside the station. Lynne answers. She tells me to stay where I am. She and Robin will come and pick me up.

I am sitting on the kerb, near the taxi rank, when a grey car with big, astonished headlights pulls into view, Robin behind the wheel. Beside him is Lynne Atwood, dressed entirely in black. Her long hair is pinned up in an extravagant bun, and she is holding a glass of red wine. When Robin brakes, she puts her glass down on the open flap of the glove compartment and shakes my hand through the window, the expression on her face at once imperious and playful. I climb into the back of the car. The interior smells of warm leather.

'Smoothly, please,' Lynne says as we leave the station. 'I don't want to spill my drink.'

On the drive back to the house, she quickly establishes that I have arrived empty-handed, and seems insulted. I feel hard done by. I have interrupted my work and travelled halfway across the country. This wasn't my idea.

That evening, on the way to the pub, I find myself walking next to Lynne. As the narrow road dips down towards a railway bridge, she gives me a cool, appraising glance.

'You know, Robin knocks you into a cocked hat,' she says.

I stare at her. 'What do you mean?'

She doesn't answer.

I swallow and look away. Most people have a sense of the different lives they might have lived, of turnings not taken, chances squandered, but in my case there is a definite 'other'. He is the person I would have been if my mother had not died, and he is always beside me, just beyond the corner of my eye. Sometimes his presence feels mocking or dismissive, at other times sympathetic, even concerned, but usually he strolls along in his own world, head high and easy in his skin, oblivious to my existence. The death of your mother hit you hard, Miriam told me once, because you were old enough to know what was going on. I asked her how she could tell that I'd been hard hit. She thought for a moment, then said, You went very quiet. This was the beginning of what Robin once called my 'inscrutability'. In a single afternoon I stopped being myself and became somebody else altogether.

Perhaps as a consequence of his disability, my father had a hunger in him, a kind of greed, and I indulged him, allowing him to replace my wishes and desires with his own. At the age of ten, I took up golf, a game he could no longer play. The war had deprived him of the chance to go to university, so I sat the scholarship exam and was awarded a place at Cambridge. He had always dreamed of sailing round the world. It's a wonder I didn't do that too. He exploited my new uncertainty, my diffidence, and I went along with it. Why? I suppose I wanted him to be proud of me. Also, since I had my health and he didn't, it would have seemed ungrateful, if not callous, to have refused him. For years, I felt that I was living on my father's behalf – or rather, that he was living through me; I became the host for his ambitious and frustrated spirit.

Unsurprisingly, perhaps, these traits or tendencies have carried over into some of my relationships with women. I tend to use the side of myself that seems the most appropriate, and temporarily discard the rest. I'm used to being what others want me to be. It comes naturally.

Unthinkingly. If a girlfriend leaves me, I don't pursue her. How can you pursue the dead? I just go quiet, turn away. Begin again.

Look at me from the outside, and you might well say what Lynne is saying. *You have no resources or convictions of your own. All you do is simulate. You're hollow, empty.* Is that what she is driving at? I can't be sure, and she isn't about to elaborate, but she appears to be gloating as we pass into the deep shadow beneath the railway bridge. She thinks she has seen through me, and – who knows? – maybe she has.

That night, when we return from the pub, Robin sits on a chair and sets his twelve-string acoustic guitar on his knee. He plays a chord, then hunches over the instrument, adjusting first one gleaming machine head, then another. The rest of us settle round the kitchen table. Lynne uncorks a bottle.

Robin starts with 'Amsterdam', a Jacques Brel classic that has been part of his repertoire for years. For the first few lines, his voice drops low. He is intimate, informative – setting the scene.

In the port of Amsterdam
Where the sailors all meet
There's a sailor who eats
Only fish heads and tails –

But it isn't long before the lyrics allow him – no, *compel* him – to cut loose. His eyes squeeze shut; his lips seem to tighten. He sings with a mixture of ferocity and yearning.

And he yells to the cook
With his mouth open wide
Hey, bring me more fish
Throw them down by my side –

From that point on, we're listening to a drunken lament, a ballad drenched in semen, piss and vomit, a hymn dragged reeking from the gutter. The song ends with five savagely strummed chords, the last of which is silenced the moment it is played as the flat of Robin's hand slams down over the strings. Our applause is long and wild. The room appears to cave outwards; the windows rattle in their frames. Luckily, the Atwoods have understanding neighbours.

The next song, 'Home', is one that Robin wrote. His voice lifts an octave as he launches, with a howl, into the first verse:

No, I won't be your son
My mother died, my father died –

When I first heard the song, I thought of Robert Mitchum's tattooed fingers in *The Night of the Hunter*, LOVE and HATE so proximate, so yoked together, that it's difficult to know where one ends and the other one begins, and as I listen to Robin singing it again I feel he has caught something of the uneasy, unruly time that we are living through. He seems to push himself to the limit in 'Home', except during the chorus, perhaps, where his voice softens, but even the softness has an edge to it, a thinly veiled viciousness, like a razor-blade wrapped in a piece of Andrex. For a while, he sounds disingenuous and plaintive, almost resigned, but his fury soon returns, the guitar appearing to accelerate towards that familiar, wailed denial: *No, I won't be your son . . .*

He's exactly the right amount of drunk tonight, not so drunk that he fluffs his chords or stumbles over words, but drunk enough to hit a note and wring every ounce of rage and anguish out of it. When he sings like this, I sometimes forget to breathe. I can't believe he's in a kitchen in Wales, with an audience of five. He should be up on stage, in the Marquee or the Roxy.

A year or two ago, Robin had a band called the Sticky Cherubs, and they played live on a beach near Seaford. It was low tide, and the waves were breaking far out, uneven lines of white unravelling, one after another. That distant, grainy roar. I have a photograph of Robin from that night. His washed-out drainpipe jeans, customized with zips, are ripped at the knee, and his white shirt hangs untucked and unbuttoned, revealing a black T-shirt that says RAPE ME. What looks like a dog's leash or a toilet-chain is wound around his neck. Both his hands clutch loosely at the microphone stand, and one foot is lifted off the ground, as though he might be about to stamp on something. His mouth is open. His eyes are dark, flat, disconnected. He's in the tight grip of the song. Behind him, part of a drum-kit, and the blurred but gritty horizontal layers of sand, sea and sky.

Robin.

'Home' is almost over. The words tell of someone staggering back to his lodgings after a night of heavy drinking. The tone is quiet, elegiac:

I will go where the old black men go
And shout in the dark
And fall into hedges
On my way home –

Robin performs some more of his own songs – 'One Hundred and Fifty Miles', and 'Dreaming' – and then Jacques Brel's 'My Death'. We whoop, clap and whistle between numbers. We don't want it to end. His voice is beginning to sound rough, though. He gulps from his glass of wine, which Lynne promptly refills.

'All right,' he says. 'Last one.'

Tom Jones's 'Delilah' is a song about betrayal, and Robin puts so much into it that it's a wonder he doesn't do himself an injury. As he sings of the revenge the man wreaks on his unfaithful wife, and the knife that silences her mocking laughter, my heart pushes high up into my chest, and I glance over at the Atwoods. Like me, they're captivated. They love Robin – the sheer size of him, the raw passion, the waywardness – and all of a sudden I think I understand why he was so eager for me to come to Wales. The cars are no more than a pretext. This is a place where he doesn't have to follow in my footsteps. This is a place he carved out for himself. He wanted to show me his new family. People who are devoted to him, thrilled by him. Proud of him.

'More,' the Atwoods shout.

Robin looks at me. Shrugs happily.

We leave on Monday morning in the more reliable of the two Rovers. Robin will pick up the other one in a few weeks' time. This seems to confirm the theory I came up with while he was singing, but I no longer care; the weekend was an adventure, just as he had promised it would be. We cruise along at fifty, the windows open wide. Smells jostle, intermingle. Buttercups and petrol. Leather. Queen Anne's lace.

As we cross the Severn bridge, I tell Robin what Lynne said while we were walking to the pub on Saturday.

He grins. 'That sounds just like her.'

I ask him what he thinks she meant.

He doesn't answer straight away. After perhaps a minute, he says that she'd probably heard too much about me. She did the same thing with him sometimes. She threw down the gauntlet. Threw it down really hard. It was a kind of test.

'She likes to tilt at windmills,' he says.

I suspect he knew that she would try and make me squirm a little. Maybe that had even been part of the agenda – a desire to see her put me in my place.

Once we are in Gloucestershire, he lets me have a turn behind the wheel. At first I am struck by the sheer tank-like weight of the old car. The steering is light, though, as if to compensate. When I press down on the accelerator, it takes a moment for the engine to assert itself, but then the whole structure gathers speed with unyielding determination. I feel unstoppable.

'What do you think?' he asks.

'It's heavy,' I say, 'but it's smooth as well. I like the way it surges.'

He looks pleased.

After ten minutes, I offer to swap places again. I can tell that he can't wait to be back in the driving-seat.

Somewhere east of Cheltenham, Robin changes into overdrive, and the gear lever comes off in his hand. Still thundering along the road, he holds up the gear lever and waves it about inside the car.

'They don't make them like they used to,' he says with a wild laugh. And then, 'No, wait. I got that the wrong way round.'

Tumbleweed

The weekend after we return from Wales, a friend called Toby drives down from London. Toby works for Texaco, as a geologist. Presumably, he helps the company in their quest for oil, though I can't believe he has found much of it; he always treats his job as such a joke. Good-looking, with blue-grey eyes and teeth so perfect that they could be American, Toby has a different girlfriend every time I see him.

When I first met Toby, he had two favourite places. One was the Chippenham, a pub in Maida Vale. We would be sitting on the dark brown carpet in my flat, then our eyes would meet and one of us would shout, Go! The Chippenham exerted such a pull on us that we would run there, even though it was half a mile away. Once we had burst, panting, through the double doors, Toby would shake a Rothman's out of its packet and flip it through the air. It was meant to land, filter first, between his lips, but the trick almost never worked. Still, Toby seemed to think it was worthwhile for the rare occasion on which it did. We would drink vodka or bottles of Pils, and if the table was free, we would play pool. Mostly, though, we talked to people. There was a burglar who would sit at the bar with an A–Z, planning his next job. There was a retired gravedigger. There were mischievous Irish nurses and stoned Jamaican bricklayers. I remember a dog that could jump as high as my shoulder. When the pub closed, we would often go back to someone's flat, cheap booze lined up along the skirting-board, and a room set aside for dancing. Punk had burned out. Ska was all the rage – bands like Selecter and the Specials.

Toby's other favourite nightspot was Toppers, and he was always trying to persuade me to go there with him. *Come on*, he would say. *The girls are really interesting*. In the end, I gave in. I followed him down Poland Street until we came to a sign with a top hat and a cane on it. Toby pressed a bell. The black door buzzed. We sat at the bar on the ground floor and drank tequila slammers. I suppose I should have guessed that the girls would all be topless. Most of them were about our age. The men were twenty or thirty years older – business types from out of town. If a girl tried to talk us into going downstairs, Toby would smile knowingly and shake his head. He wasn't falling for that one. The only time he'd ever been down there, he'd found himself drinking champagne. He wasn't sure how it had happened. It had cost him an arm and a leg.

It's no great surprise when Toby announces, half an hour after arriving in Eastbourne, that his first priority is to sample the nightlife. He wants some action, he says.

'Well,' Robin says, 'I suppose there's Bilbo Baggins . . .'

Toby looks wary.

'That's what it's called,' Robin explains. 'Everyone in there's about sixteen.'

'Sounds good,' Toby says.

I reach for the local paper. 'Or there's Shimmers,' I say. 'A Select Discotheque for Select People.'

'I'm select.' Toby tosses a Rothman's in the rough direction of his mouth. It bounces off his chin and drops to the floor.

'What about the organist?' Robin says.

Toby studies him through exhaled smoke, both eyebrows raised.

'The pier's resident organist, Mr Music,' I say, reading from the paper, 'is back for his twelfth season . . .'

Robin and I have already been to the bar at the end of the pier. We sat in the corner with our pints of lager while Mr Music played instrumental versions of famous top-ten hits, and OAPs shuffled round the dance floor, hands waggling in the air above their heads. *Time for another drink, isn't it?* Mr Music would say between numbers. *Me, I'm sticking to the hard stuff. Lemonade.* He laughed at all his own jokes. His suit was the colour of porridge.

'He does a lovely "Puppet on a String",' Robin says. 'Really lovely.'

'No,' Toby says. 'I don't think so.'

We drive up to the top of the Downs in Toby's car, stopping at the pub on Beachy Head for a beer and a game of pool. On my way to the toilets, I pass two black plastic bin bags that have been dumped in the passage, and they remind me of what happened earlier in the week. We had agreed that Dad's clothes should be donated to the charity shop in Old Town, and I had volunteered for the task. One afternoon, when the house was quiet, I opened the airing cupboard. There, on the wooden slats, were his shirts, his socks, his string vests and his underpants, everything folded, everything warm. I lifted out the nearest pile and placed it in a bin bag. I had to work fast, afraid of what I might think if I allowed myself to think, afraid of what I might feel. At times, I seemed to sense Dad watching me with a look of bemusement. *What are you doing with my clothes?* Once the airing cupboard was empty, I loaded the bags into the boot of the Renault and slammed the lid. That was the hard part over – or so I thought.

When I pulled up outside the charity shop, there were no lights on. Then I realized what day it was. Wednesday. Early closing. Hands on the steering wheel, I stared through the windscreen. I couldn't bring myself to take Dad's clothes back home with me. I couldn't bear to go through this again. The charity shop was double-fronted, I noticed, with a kind of porch between the two display windows. If I stacked the bags in that small, sheltered place, they would be protected from the elements, and the people who ran the shop would find them in the morning.

Throwing glances left and right, as though engaged in some criminal activity, I carried the bags over the road and heaped them against the shop's front door. When I was finished, I hurried back to the car. The bags looked more visible than I had imagined they would. What if the dustmen thought they were rubbish? Drops of rain appeared on the windscreen – delicately, magically, as though conjured by the glass itself. His shirts with their worn collars and frayed cuffs, his socks darned with wool that was never the right colour. The fact that his clothes had been mended, cared for, made to last – and now they were out there in the dark, the cold . . . I lean on the sink in the Gents. My face floats on the green surface of the mirror, mournful, soggy-looking, and I remember how the rain grew heavier, and how I went on sitting in the car. These endless goodbyes, and every one of them mismanaged.

Later, as Toby drives us back to the town centre, he flips another cigarette towards his mouth. For once, he catches it between his teeth.

'That's the first time in how long?' I say, an edge in my voice.

Toby stamps on the brakes. 'Do you want to walk?'

'Sorry,' I say. 'It's not you.'

We have drinks in Bilbo Baggins and more drinks in Diplocks on Terminus Road, and then, when all the pubs have closed, we climb a narrow flight of stairs to Ziggy's. We sit at a see-through table shaped like a surfboard. The DJ puts on Billy Joel's 'Uptown Girl', a song I've always hated. The dance floor is packed but lifeless. I feel a kind of rage or turmoil gathering inside me. I down two vodkas. Light a cigarette. Toby's chatting up a blonde. Words glisten on the front of her pink T-shirt. Action, I mutter to myself. The watery drinks, the dreary dancing. Now they're playing 'A Flock of Seagulls'. Christ. The surfboard bristles with bottles and ashtrays. A glass glows in the ultraviolet; it looks so white and two-dimensional that it could have been drawn with a piece of chalk. All right, that's it. I've had enough. Leaning forwards, I reach out and sweep the whole lot on to the floor. There's a huge crash and then a splintering and a girl at the bar bends double, as if someone just punched her in the stomach. Another girl has brought her hands up to her cheeks. No music suddenly, just a silence that is choppy, swirly. A bit like being under the sea. Near the shore, though. Waves tumbling over my head.

'I always wanted to do that,' I say, but not to anybody in particular.

Two bouncers seize me. One white, one black.

'You're very symmetrical,' I say.

Hands gripping me under the arms, they haul me through the club, then down the stairs. There are three of us. It's a tight squeeze.

'Not easy, is it,' I say, 'throwing someone out?'

I'm chatty now. My mood's improved no end.

They fling me across the pavement, then stand over me, brawny forearms dangling. I feel like I'm in a western. They should have six-guns and star-shaped metal badges that say SHERIFF. I glance at the road behind me. Where's the tumbleweed?

'Don't ever,' the white one says, 'don't – fucking – *ever* come back here again, all right?'

Robin appears in the doorway, face tinted blue by the neon above the entrance. 'Don't worry, he won't,' he says. 'Because this place stinks – of shit.'

The black bouncer swings round, levelling a stubby finger. 'And you. Don't you never come back neither.'

I lie back in the gutter, laughter bubbling inside me. *Oh no. Banned from Ziggy's.* The night seems to stagger. It's made of big dark blocks that don't quite fit together.

Robin helps me to my feet.

'You see it sometimes, don't you,' I say, 'in films, but you can't imagine doing it.'

'It was loud. People screamed.'

'Was it?' I rub my elbow. 'It felt good. Really good.'

Robin looks off up the street, towards the seafront, and then looks back at me. 'I'm usually the one who does things like that.'

'I know. Makes a change, doesn't it?'

Toby crosses the pavement. 'You could have said something. You know, like, I'm tired. Or, Can we go now?'

'Shut up, Toby,' Robin says.

On the way home, Robin and I sit in the back of Toby's

car. I lean my head against the headrest. Each passing street lamp makes a photocopy of my face. I watch as Robin reaches into the gap between the side of Toby's head and the half-open window and lets the slipstream snatch his cigarette.

'You were like a brother back there,' I tell him. 'That's what brothers do.'

'I *am* your brother.'

I smile.

This is probably the first time Robin has ever taken care of me. In the past it was always the other way round. He even said it to me once: *You had to be our mother, didn't you, after she died?* For years I have found responsibility exhausting – the very word exhausts me – but now, suddenly, I feel younger than Robin, and light, infinitely light, so much so that I nearly float out of the window and off into the gaudy, lurching fairground of the night.

Little Black Joe

Uncle Joe died in September 1988, barely two years after my one and only meeting with him. I was living in Los Angeles at the time, but Frank sent me Xeroxes of the pen-and-ink pictures Beth had drawn after the funeral. They showed Joe in a coffin, surrounded by a horde of bearded men in baggy trousers and sandals.

On my return to England, I learned that Joe's funeral had taken place in a cemetery in Walsall, and that he had been carried to his grave by members of the mosque where he had worshipped. No women attended, except for Miriam and Beth. Islamic law demanded that they remove their shoes; they had to stand on the wet grass in their stockinged feet. Frank was asked if he would like to say a few words. He declined. Though Joe was his brother, Frank felt marginal, excluded – a bystander rather than a true participant. According to Beth, Joe was lying on his side in the open air. His coffin, she said, was made out of fruit crates. He looked pale, unusually so, but she was able to recognize him by the slight indentation in the tip of his nose. Though the sky was overcast that day, a shaft of sunlight angled down on to Joe's face, and this was thought to be a good sign.

When I next spoke to Frank, he told me that the chapel at Tonbridge had burned down within hours of Joe's death, and that he believed this was Joe's doing. Joe had been expelled from the school. Now he had taken his revenge.

'Well, it's certainly in character,' I said.

I was thinking of the army building that had gone up in flames in Korea, but I also knew that Joe had been thrown out of his digs in Tamworth for regularly setting fire to the contents of his waste-paper basket. And then there were his various tirades against the residents of Penndale Lodge. *You're going to burn in hell, the lot of you.*

Some years later, in the mid-nineties, I had the idea of basing a novel on Joe's life, but my grasp on his story was sketchy at best, and I drove up to Frank and Miriam's house to see whether they could fill in any of the blanks. As usual, Frank dodged certain questions and dredged up anecdotes I had heard before, and occasionally, if pressed, he would shriek, 'I *don't know*, I *can't remember*.' It occurred to me that he might be jealous of my interest in his brother – why couldn't I show more interest in *him*? – and, feeling chastened, I sat in the kitchen and asked about his Japanese childhood, his war-time experiences, and his struggles at the mill.

Not long before I left, and quite unexpectedly, he handed me an A4 envelope containing photocopies of two letters Joe had sent from South America. 'Well,' he said, looking away from me, 'you wanted to know what he was like . . .'

Written on headed airmail paper, and dated 18 February 1951, the first letter was more than forty pages long. Joe's handwriting tilted forwards in a hurried scrawl, and there were places where the ink had smudged; I could sense the humidity, his pen gripped in fingers that were slippery with sweat. When Joe landed in Colombia to take up his job with the London Bank of South America, he had felt, he said, 'like someone who'd been away for a long time and had finally come back'. I put the letter down, startled by what I'd just read. I had felt exactly the same when I arrived in Italy in 1982. I had given up everything – my job, my flat – and I was going to write. After driving down through France, I spent the night in a small white hotel on a rocky promontory a few miles west of Cannes – a miracle that it was open; everywhere else had closed for the winter – and when I crossed the border at Ventimiglia the next morning, my heart seemed to expand. I hadn't expected such a rush of happiness. The empty *autostrada,* the glitter of the Mediterranean off to the right and far below. My first Italian service station, where I stood at a zinc counter and drank a cappuccino. It felt like a home-coming. Home isn't the place you grow up in, or the place where your parents live. Home is a place you come across by chance, if you're lucky.

I picked up Joe's letter again. 'Sounds odd, doesn't it,' he had written, 'but that's the way it was.' No, Joe, I thought, not odd at all. I could see him stepping off the plane, the night so lush and muggy that it seemed to wrap its arms around him. Downtown Bogotá. The Green Room at the Hotel Granada. The Copacabana Club. Girls deliberately brushing against him as they passed him in the street. Flashed glances. The looseness of everything. This is it, he must have thought. This is it – for ever.

Within a few weeks, he had assembled 'a wonderful set of friends and companions', all of them Colombian. He claimed they loved and respected him more than any Englishman they had ever come across, and that they accepted him as one of their own, not just because he spoke the language fluently, but because he willingly adopted many of their attitudes and customs. He also happened to have a naturally dark complexion. His mother, Pim, had always referred to him, affectionately, as 'little black Joe', and Joe himself, in his letters to Frank, hypothesized that there must be Latin blood in the family, 'which has come out particularly in me personally'. Smiling, I remembered how Frank had once told me, with great relish, that we were partly descended from the Aborigines. Granny Ellis – my great-grandmother – was half Aborigine, he had assured me, being the love-child of an illicit and scandalous union between an Ellis woman and an Aboriginal man. But there was also Beth's startling revelation, on a recent visit, that Frank's grandfather had been 'a black man'. She had seen a photograph of him, she said, and he was 'distinctly very, *very* dark'. Most telling for Beth was the fact that Frank had been unable – or unwilling – to trace the family on his father's side, whereas on his mother's side, apparently, he'd got all the way back to John of Gaunt. Whatever the reason for Joe's skin colour, people in Bogotá were always mistaking him for a local. He described how an American woman had approached him at the club. 'How is it,' she asked, 'that you speak such good English?' According to Joe, his reply – 'I *am* English' – was delivered with a caustic edge, but I suspected that he found that kind of misapprehension flattering.

There were three other Englishmen at the bank who were in their twenties, but they steadfastly refused to mix with Colombians outside the office. 'Poor things!' Joe wrote. 'How much they missed!' His father, James

Gausden, had spent more than thirty years in the Far East, and James – or 'Gentleman Jim', as he was sometimes known – had made a point of immersing himself in Japanese culture and tradition. Joe, too, plunged headlong into his new environment, but unlike his father he had a reckless streak and a profound disdain for convention. In expatriate society, such behaviour could be dangerous, a fact of which he was not unaware. 'If any little bit of scandal gets around or in the papers,' he wrote, 'the man is ruined – quite literally ruined.'

While dining at his boarding-house, Joe met a Colombian from 'a very good family'. A few days later, he ran into the man again, on Avenida de la República, and the man invited him to the house of a friend who lived nearby. They drank superior rum, and the man's friend played the piano and sang opera and popular Spanish and Colombian songs. He also had a number of female companions who were considered 'reliable'. Joe became a regular visitor to this lavish Spanish-colonial-style house. There would be eating, drinking, dancing *amasisado* – or 'belly-to-belly', as he explained, 'with the leg of the man between the legs of the woman' – and later there would be sex. The men introduced him to several acquaintances of theirs, two of whom lived in the upper fringes of the city, beneath the mountains. In their atmospheric apartment, with its dark, heavily furnished rooms, they showed him albums filled with pictures of half-naked girls, all of whom were readily available. The parties would continue on into the small hours – Joe would often stay the night and turn up at the bank the following day without having gone home at all – but since everything was happening in exclusive neighbourhoods, and behind closed doors, his reputation remained intact.

And then, as Joe put it, he 'got into a jam with a tart'. Shortly after arriving in Bogotá, he had picked up a girl near the Calle Real, not knowing she had served prison sentences for blackmail, drugs and theft. Almost a year later, he had the misfortune to run into the girl again on his way to work. From then on, she began to accost him outside the bank. She told him, among other things, that she'd had a child, and that he was the father. He bribed her to stay away, but the matter had already come to the attention of his superiors. Before reassigning him to a more obscure branch of the bank in Guayaquil, the manager gave Joe a lecture about his conduct. 'I laughed openly,' Joe wrote, 'right in his face.' Joe had lost interest in his job, and had sorely tried the patience of his employers, upon whose good will he was dependent, and yet, at the same time, he was telling Frank that he wanted to settle in South America, and that he didn't have the slightest intention of returning home.

Both the letters Frank had photocopied for me had been posted in Guayaquil – after Joe's demotion, in other words. In this remote, unsophisticated city, Joe had far less opportunity to indulge his vices, and deeply regretted his removal from Bogotá, where life had been such an endless round of pleasure. Apart from the Phoenix Club and the Hotel Crillon, there was nowhere to go, and before too long he found himself drawn to the red-light district, which even he admitted was 'extremely sordid'. As a precaution, he adopted a Spanish name, posing as an unemployed Colombian, but somebody saw through him and once again he was caught up in a web of intrigue and blackmail. Within a month, he was arrested and charged with offences so 'vile and shameful' that he couldn't bring himself to go into any detail. Rather than pay off the two detectives who appeared at his hotel, he insisted they escort him to the bank, where his superiors were eventually able to sort the matter out with the chief of police. 'The boss was furious,' Joe wrote, 'and said that if I was ever involved in any kind of scandal again, whether I was innocent or not, I would be thrown out of the bank on the spot and sent back to England.'

Which is precisely what happened, of course.

Within a year of writing the letters, Joe was deported from South America. He claimed the charges that had been brought against him were fabrications – 'the most filthy calumnies' – but as he himself had already pointed out, the whole question of innocence had become irrelevant. Since Frank was vague on the subject – he either couldn't, or wouldn't, tell me the full story – it was hard to know what to believe, but it seemed Joe had been co-operating with, or even orchestrating, his destiny from the very beginning, and I imagined his downfall had more to do with a long history of rebellious behaviour than with any one particular event.

I pictured him on the flight back to England, staring through the window as the plane banked to the northeast, the continent he had fallen in love with seeming for a few moments to move closer, to press itself against him, a last slow dance, but his one-line reference from the bank would have been in his pocket all the while, like a millstone. Like a death sentence. Did he realize that he had wasted the best chance he would ever be given? Did he sense that the odds were now stacked against him? 'It was a terrible blow,' Frank said of his brother's deportation. 'He was very upset by it and shaken. Very bitter. He never recovered, really.'

From that point on, Joe contrived an ever-tightening

cage for himself. He sold his comfortable house in Birmingham and bought one that was smaller. Then he swapped the smaller house for something smaller still. He moved into digs by the railway arches in Tamworth. There were dead-end jobs. Months of living rough. A two-up two-down in Whitmore Reans, the poorest part of Wolverhampton. That threadbare, smoke-filled lounge in Penndale Lodge. A coffin made of fruit crates on the side of a hill. I still had so many questions, and wished I had put them to him when I had the chance. But you don't, do you? It's only when people have died that you realize what you wanted to know. Only when they cannot answer.

Years later, while staying with Frank and Miriam, I happened to mention Joe's funeral. 'It was completely foreign,' Miriam told me. 'More like Baghdad than Birmingham.'

That same weekend, thinking of visiting the grave, I asked Frank where Joe was buried. He could no longer remember.

Beautiful Day

I stand by Dad's bedroom window. Outside, the cherry trees are in full bloom, their branches loaded with extravagantly frothy pale pink blossoms. From somewhere nearby comes the sleepy drone of a motor mower. In the distance, above the hedge, are the Downs, the top of the ridge lost in the heat haze. We have been living in the house for almost four months.

I hear a voice in the garden and peer down. Below me, on the lawn, are Vivian and Greta. Vivian is wearing a long-sleeved T-shirt and jeans, and she is propped on her elbows with her legs stretched out in front of her. Greta sits nearby, a sun hat at a jaunty angle on her head. Just then, Ralph emerges from the sitting-room in a white shirt and white trousers. He has rolled his sleeves back to the elbow. His arms are even paler than his face.

He kneels down, chin almost touching his right knee, and says something to Greta. His hair is receding, revealing the widow's peak he had when he was born. It looks as if he might go bald even before I do. He kisses Greta, then turns and speaks to Vivian. I can see how proud he is, and how happy, and if I stay where I am, half hidden by the curtain, it's only because I would like to understand a bit more about their lives, and what goes on in Paradise, behind that sealed door. Arranged on the grass, and barely moving, they might be sitting for a portrait, and as I watch they suddenly seem vulnerable, exposed. To have a family is like asking for it. Tempting fate. There's just so much that can go wrong, and there isn't a lock in the world that can protect you.

I step forwards into the open window and lean on the sill. Still crouching, Ralph is alive to the movement and glances up at me, over his shoulder. In that instant, my viewpoint alters, and I see myself as he must see me, positioned high above him, like some kind of predator. *How long have you been there? Have you been spying on us? I wouldn't try anything if I were you.*

Perhaps I'm being melodramatic.

I take a deep breath of the blossom-scented air, then let it out again. 'Beautiful day,' I say.

Ralph looks away into the garden. 'It's perfect.'

Vivian reaches for Greta.

Letter from Shanghai

A few months after visiting Uncle Frank and looking at his pictures of Ralph, I sat at my kitchen table in Barcelona with a blank sheet of paper in front of me. The thermometer on the wall said 35° Celsius, and my wrist kept sticking to the plastic tablecloth. Outside, in the small, tiled courtyard, the marquesa's spade-shaped leaves gleamed in the humid air. I was trying to write to Ralph, but I knew so little about him that I was having trouble finding a tone of voice. I had already crumpled up my first three efforts.

On my fourth attempt, I began by reminding him of what he had once said – namely that if I ever wanted to contact him, I should do so in writing. So here I am, I said, writing. I paused for perhaps a minute, then bent over the paper again. It was possible, I went on, that he had interpreted my silence as respect – I had allowed him the privacy he had insisted on – but if he looked at it from another angle he might equally see it as indifference. In obeying him as I had, in giving up so easily, had I confirmed some theory he had about me? Had I showed him

that I didn't care? I sat back. *Did* I care? It was difficult to
know. I had become accustomed to not seeing him, to
doing without. It wasn't a hardship exactly. More like a
habit. Nineteen years had gone by since we had spoken,
twenty-two since we had stood in the same room.

The last time I had talked to my wife, Kate, about the
idea of getting in touch with Ralph, she had said, You
know, you really should have agreed to be his best man. I
sighed. We had been over this ground before, but Kate
could never quite believe that I had turned Ralph down.
Didn't it ever occur to you, she'd said once, that he might
have cut himself off from the world to such an extent that
he still saw you as one of the people closest to him? Didn't
you realize that he might have had nobody else to turn to?
I shook my head, but said nothing. Your brother's supposed to be someone you can call on, she said, someone
you can *rely* on, no matter *what* the circumstances. Maybe
I was tired of being relied on, I said. Maybe I wanted to get
away from all that. Well, you certainly chose your
moment, she said. In times of need, she went on, you
should be able to count on family. She paused. Or perhaps
he was reaching out in the only way he knew how, she said
slowly. Perhaps that letter he sent you was an olive branch
of sorts. I never thought of that, I said. But now, of
course – with hindsight . . . Kate had given me a steady
look. I know, I murmured. I should have said yes.

If I was finally writing to Ralph, though, it wasn't out of
guilt. While examining the photographs the previous
December, a thought had occurred to me, and I decided to
put that thought straight into the letter. It would be
strange, wouldn't it, I said, if we were to die without ever
setting eyes on each other again? Yes, I might want to try
and unravel the mystery of our estrangement, and I might

even feel the need to apologize to him, but the urge simply to see him outweighed all that. I leaned over the paper again. He was living in Shanghai, I said, which was a place I had always longed to visit. If I were to happen to pass through the city at some point in the future, would he meet me for a drink?

I put my pen down and read through what I had written. I thought I had struck more or less the right note. I had been direct, though not intrusive. I wasn't suggesting we should start living in one another's pockets; I had merely presented him with a space he could walk into, if he so wished.

The day after posting the letter, I flew to Australia, and when I returned home two weeks later I found a white envelope in my letter box. The stamps were Chinese. It looked as though Ralph had written back almost immediately, which seemed like a good sign – unless, of course, it was a snub; he might be telling me to bugger off, as Uncle Joe used to do when family members showed up on his doorstep in Wolverhampton. Still, at least I could say I had tried. I turned the letter in my hands, but found no clue as to what kind of reply it might contain. I held the envelope to my nose and got a whiff of fabric. Not new, though. Second-hand. Was that what Shanghai smelled like? I had flown overnight from Sydney, with a four-hour lay-over in Frankfurt, and I needed sleep, but I would read Ralph's letter first.

Dear Rupert, it began, *Wow – that was a surprise.*

The tone was sincere throughout, and friendly, so much so that I fell to wondering why the estrangement had lasted as long as it had. I returned to the top of the page and saw that he too seemed bewildered. *When I read your letter, it was weird because what I said some twenty years ago sounds all a bit, I don't know, dramatic* ... After the 1987 phone call, I had assumed that any attempt to make contact would be interpreted as an aggressive act, and if, during the years that followed, I ever imagined a scenario in which I showed up outside Ralph's house and rang the bell, the door would always be answered by Vivian, and she would be aiming a loaded shotgun at me. Dramatic, yes – a word Ralph had used himself – but not, I felt, beyond the bounds of possibility.

A correspondence began. There would be days, even weeks, between e-mails. At least the lines of communication were open, though. Ralph's personality would shift from offbeat to businesslike – I had no real purchase on it – but what didn't seem to be in any doubt was his willingness to see me.

The following summer, as my travel plans took shape, I suggested that maybe we could meet twice – once to break the ice, since it had been a long time, and then again because I had some questions I hoped he could help me with. Now our reunion was only a few weeks away, I was adopting the cautious tone that he had used at the beginning of our correspondence: 'break the ice', for instance, was a phrase I remembered from his letter. He promptly became playful. *Questions?* he said. *Sounds like an interview.* And then, *What's all this about it's been a long time? It's only twenty-three years or so* ... By early December, though, just days before my departure, he had taken to reassuring me. *Listen, I know it's been a while, but you know who I am and I know who you are, so it'll be fine.*

Did I, though?

Did he?

Like a Reservoir

The weekend before I'm due to go on holiday with Hanne, Robin and I have a party in the garden. Temperatures have been up in the eighties for several days; the lawn is studded with daisies, and a heady perfume lifts off the roses that sprawl across the garage wall. Robin puts his wind-up gramophone on the stone plinth where the statue of the rabbit used to be and starts singing along to crackly recordings of George Formby, Noël Coward, Douglas Byng and Marlene Dietrich. *Oh – see what the boys in the back-room will have* . . . Bernard appears, immaculate as always in a dark green jacket, a white shirt, and a thin black tie. Robin tries to persuade him to join in. Come on, Bernard. I bet you've got a lovely voice. Bernard giggles. No, no. I'm afraid it's not true. Jenny Martin drops in. So does a family from Lewes. As darkness falls, we light a bonfire behind the hedge. We wrap sausages and potatoes in silver foil and bake them in the ashes.

Later, I find Robin sitting outside the kitchen, his back against the wall. Next to him is Lola, one of the girls from Lewes. She has dyed copper-coloured hair, and her full lips glisten in the dark. I settle on the flagstones nearby, which still glow with the heat of the day. Lola is gazing at Robin, but he is staring up into the sky and doesn't realize. Suddenly, all I can think about is kissing her. She's only sixteen, though – she might even be fifteen – and anyway, it's Robin she fancies. When I pointed Lola out to a doctor friend of ours a while ago, he glanced at her, then sucked some air in through his teeth and muttered, Jailbait.

I notice Robin's twelve-string guitar leaning against the glasshouse. 'Why don't you sing? I love it when you sing.'

He gives me a look.

'I do,' I say.

'Not drunk enough,' he says.

Later still, with a Bowie album playing on the stereo, I stand on my own in the kitchen garden. The fire is so hot that my face feels glazed. Sparks shower upwards, past the apple trees; the black air seems to snuff them out. Near the end of 'Moonage Daydream', the guitar soars like a kind of heartache, then tightens and accelerates, each note a curved blade cutting into the soft, dark folds of the night, and I think of the last postcard I sent Hanne. *I still feel very sad about Dad, not deep down, but just under the surface, very still and huge, like a reservoir . . .*

Reservoir, I hear her murmur. What is reservoir?

I fly to Munich on the last Monday in June. Hanne picks me up in her yellow VW and we drive through the night, over the Alps and down on to the northern plains of Italy, the *autostrada* slick and trembling in the heat. Three days later, we arrive in Positano, checking into the hotel where I stayed the previous summer. The price of a room has doubled. The next morning, when we walk down to the beach, we discover that access is now controlled; there are rows of brand-new colour-coded sunloungers, and you have to pay a daily rate. I look for a fisherman called Salvatore. He always wore a white singlet and baggy dark blue shorts, and his calf muscles bulged like a couple of roast chickens. I had lunch with him once, on a trestle table by the sea. We ate that morning's catch – grilled white fish, with bright wedges of lemon – and when I told him I had fallen for a girl from Hamburg he let out a raucous belly-laugh. I stop at various bars and shops and ask for him by name. Most people seem to know him, but their answers are vague, contradictory. *He was here last week. I saw him. He's moved. He's working somewhere else. Where? I'm not sure. Further down the coast.* His absence takes some of the joy out of our return.

That evening we order our usual drinks – Campari soda for Hanne, chilled Cinzano Bianco for me. I knock my glass over almost as soon as it arrives. It was the table, I say. It's got a slope to it. We have been spilling our drinks ever since the holiday began, so much so that we are keeping a tally. We have turned our clumsiness into a game, inventing excuses each time it happens, but I can't help feeling that it must be significant, that some sort of truth is being hinted at. The waiter brings me another Cinzano. Every now and then, my eyes move to the narrow street outside. A part of me is longing for Salvatore to walk past, and I find myself thinking of Willard Bowen, a man I met in New York in 1976.

'The same thing happened with him,' I tell Hanne. 'He just vanished.'

I first saw Willard Bowen in a grocery store on Seventh Avenue. I was trying to decide which kind of orange juice to buy – Minute Maid or Tropicana – when a raspy voice behind me said, Get the Minute Maid. Turning, I caught a glimpse of a man disappearing round the end of an aisle. When I walked out of the store five minutes later, he was standing on the corner. Unshaven, with cropped grey hair, he wore a short-sleeved shirt and loose grey trousers. Pulled down low over his eyes was a visor with a see-through green plastic brim, which made me think of old-time newspapermen. We started talking. I told him I couldn't afford the $9 a night I was paying at the International Hostel on Riverside Drive, and that I was looking for something cheaper. He said I could stay with him and his family. No strings attached, he said, licking his dry lips. I thanked him, but said I'd go on looking.

Two days later, as chance would have it, we met again. I was sitting outside the New York Post Office when he showed up at the bottom of the steps. By then, I had become dispirited. The $20-a-week boarding-houses I had found all seemed to be run by tattooed amputees in wheel-chairs, or gloomy, sweat-stained perverts. Thin hardboard partitions separated one box-like room from another. Cockroaches skittered across the lino floors, and the beds – if you could call them beds – were bustling with lice. As one proprietor told me, in a narrow, unlit hall, *People only come here to fucking die.* Willard repeated his offer, and I decided to take him up on it. His 'family' consisted of a nephew, Joe, who walked with a limp – he had been shot in the foot while serving in Vietnam – and Russell, a twenty-year-old runaway from Georgia. Willard had found Russell sleeping rough on a park bench, and was drawing social security on his behalf. I lived with them for seven weeks, first in one room on West 23rd Street, then in a cold-water apartment on Tenth Avenue, next to a gas station. Willard would start drinking at ten in the morning – beer with vodka chasers. To begin with, I would go with him, usually to the nearest Blarney Rose. Later, I would explore the city. In those days, Manhattan had a jittery, feral atmosphere – especially in Hell's Kitchen, our new neighbourhood. You learned to walk as if you knew where you were going. You never looked at a map. In the evenings, we sat on the fire escape, Willard smoking a cigar. Once, Joe sang Elvis songs. He didn't have a guitar, but his voice was so powerful it made the walls vibrate. Russell almost never spoke. I'm going out, I heard him say to Willard once, and then he was gone for three days. That summer Jimmy Carter received the Democratic nomination, and when delegates flew in for the convention, all the drug-dealing and prostitution was shunted west on to Ninth and Tenth Avenues in an attempt to preserve the city's reputation. Black girls gave truck drivers blow jobs in the twenty-four-hour parking-lot opposite our building. Junkies shot up in broad daylight. A pimp was stabbed. Sirens wailed, blue police lights whirled. As Willard said, Who needs TV? Though it was hot – a muggy, steamy, almost vegetable heat – we slept fully clothed on bare mattresses; there was a bath in the kitchen, but I don't remember using it. Once, in the night, I woke to find Willard fumbling at the buttons on my jeans. Willard, I said, don't. Oh, come on, he murmured. I turned on to my side, away from him. You said no strings. He slunk back to the window, muttering. I felt petty, ungrateful. He had opened up a whole new world for me. What had I given him?

By August, I had become restless. America was out there, waiting: Los Angeles, San Francisco – Nashville, Tennessee. Willard tried to persuade me not to go. He wanted to adopt me as his son. He would get the proper

forms, he said. Do it legally. He was serious. The radio
was tuned to a local New York station, and Elton John
and Kiki Dee were singing 'Don't Go Breaking My
Heart', one of the big hits of the summer. I don't know, I
said. What about my father? Willard told me he had a
farm in Kentucky. He had money too. Look. His bank
statement showed a balance in excess of $300,000. But I
couldn't quite believe what he was showing me – and
anyway, I was desperate to travel. Sitting by the fire
escape, the gritty New York light behind him, Willard
shook his small shaved head. I'll come back, I told him. In
three months' time. He shook his head again, then spat
through the casement. You won't come back. I will, I said.
I promise. As a sign of my good faith, I left a cardboard
box with him. Inside were a pair of black patent-leather
shoes, a transistor radio, and a paperback copy of *Riders
in the Chariot*. Willard didn't find my gesture even faintly
convincing. He thought these were things I had no further
use for.

In early November, I caught a Greyhound bus from Fort
Lauderdale, arriving in New York at seven in the morning.
The smell of neat spirits and toasted pretzels was so familiar that walking out of Port Authority felt like returning
home, but several months had passed, and the air now
had a vicious winter snap to it. I buttoned my jacket and
hurried over to Tenth Avenue, my sense of urgency increasing with every step. I was eager to prove to Willard that I
was as good as my word – and I had stories for him too. I
knew he would like the one about me losing my virginity
on red satin sheets in New Orleans. And the one about me
going to a party in the Hollywood Hills with the actors
who played the inmates in *One Flew over the Cuckoo's
Nest*. And the one about me finding 8,000 pesos on the

tarmac outside the bus station in Mexico City. But when I pressed his buzzer, nobody answered. I went looking for the building's super. He was in the basement, fixing the boiler. He had sticking-up white hair and a stomach that wobbled like a balloon full of water. They moved out, he told me. Couple months ago. I asked if he knew where they had gone. He threw his cigarette butt on the floor, then rubbed his swollen belly. Last I heard, the guy was up on 110th Street, he said, selling newspapers.

Feeling like a detective, I jumped on a C train going uptown. Wide and busy, 110th Street ran along the south side of Harlem, and there were newspaper vendors on almost every corner. I worked my way from west to east, describing Willard Bowen as best I could. Sounds like a bum, one of the vendors said, and I thought of Willard's bank statement and wondered whether it was real. In my first hour I must have spoken to fifteen or twenty men, but none of them had seen anybody who answered to my description.

I was about to give up when a wiry little man with the lean, sharp face of a ferret told me he had talked to Willard two weeks ago. He couldn't say where Willard was living, though. I mentioned Joe and Russell. No, he didn't remember nobody like that. I thanked him, then moved away. Half a block later, I came to a standstill. Hundreds of people, all moving in different directions. We'd had two chance meetings, Willard and I. This, surely, was the moment for the third. But no, nothing. What would a real detective do? He would check every bar in the neighbourhood, and every grocery store. He would knock on doors, ask questions. He would stick at the task for as long as it took. I didn't have much time, though. I was flying back to England in a day or two.

As I walked reluctantly towards the nearest subway entrance, I wondered if it would occur to Willard that I had looked for him. When Christmas came, and I still hadn't appeared, what would he think? Would he realize that he had made it almost impossible for me to find him, or would he conclude, bitterly, that his prediction had been accurate, and that when I left the apartment on Tenth Avenue I'd had no intention of returning? Would he assume that I had tired of him? That I'd had better offers? That, in the end, I simply didn't care enough? You won't come back, he had said. You'll never come back. But I did. He wasn't there.

Three years later, in New York again, I went through the phone directory and found a *Bowen, W.* Willard hadn't had a phone in 1976. Why would he have one now? All the same, I dialled the number. There was no reply. I called several times during my visit, but nobody ever answered. I left New York believing he was dead.

'It's a sad story,' Hanne says.

'I should have gone on looking.'

'You tried.'

I shake my head. 'Not hard enough.'

We say goodbye to Positano. Back along the Amalfi coast, then south through the suburbs of Naples. Dust and rubble everywhere. Circus posters hang in tatters under flyovers, and the roads are so pitted with potholes that Hanne has to drive in second gear. Turning east, we make for the Gargano. It's July now; the land is white with heat.

Another café-bar. When my drink arrives, condensation mists the glass. The last of the sun tints the upper storeys of the houses opposite. Down here, in the shade, I gaze at the olives on their saucer. Such an eerie colour. They could be stones from a broken necklace – pieces of beryl or green amethyst. Hanne knocks her Campari over. There was a flying insect, she says. Did you see?

After three weeks, Hanne drops me at Munich airport. She can't stay long; she starts work tomorrow, and it's a five-hour drive to West Berlin. Though we haven't talked about splitting up, or even mentioned it as a possibility, I feel an intense nostalgia as she walks back to her car. Our holiday in Italy has altered nothing; there is still the crude, blunt fact of my father's death, which hasn't just interrupted our life together but has also, somehow, called the whole relationship into question.

As I board the plane, I notice that the sky has darkened above the main terminal building. It is only midday, but lights show in all the windows. Half an hour goes by. My fellow passengers are shifting in their seats. Then a strange sound begins above my head, as if dozens of people are attacking the roof of the plane with hammers. A woman screams. I peer out of my window. Hailstones the size of apricots are bouncing off the tarmac. The noise is so loud that I can't hear what the man next to me is saying. When the storm has passed, the captain makes an announcement. He is very sorry, but the aircraft has almost certainly been damaged. We will have to disembark. As we traipse back to the terminal, I glance at the plane. Its fuselage is dented all over, symmetrically, like a golf ball.

In Departures, the roof is leaking, and there are puddles everywhere. A large woman in a floral-print dress loses her footing. It takes two men to help her up. She has twisted her ankle, though, and cannot walk. The British have started drinking. I hope Hanne's all right. I wish I could call her, but she'll still be on the motorway. I find a paper and try to read. We are told a replacement aircraft is being flown in, though no one knows when it is due. There are outbursts of defiant singing from the British. A paunchy, balding man in an England football shirt gives me a wink. Don't mention the war, he says. Later, he slips on a wet patch, and his bag of duty-free goes flying. The whole building reeks of Bacardi after that. It's hours before we're able to board another plane. I don't reach Eastbourne till midnight.

On my first morning back, Robin tells me that Ralph sold Dad's bureau desk while he, Robin, was visiting friends in Lewes. He says he'd had his eye on the desk for ages; he would have been happy to pay each of us our share of what it was worth. Although I sympathize with him, and agree that Ralph ought not to have acted without consult-ing us, the loss of the desk doesn't affect me. But then he mentions that Ralph has also sold the Braque lithograph that used to hang above the fireplace in Dad's bedroom. An auction house called Edgar Horn has given us £2,000 for it.

'But that's only four hundred each,' I say to Ralph, when he returns from work that evening. 'It would have been better to keep it in the family.' Even as I speak, I realize I am sounding just like Dad.

'It seemed like a fair price.' Ralph is avoiding my eyes, but he doesn't look guilty, let alone apologetic.

'I wish you'd asked.'

'You weren't here.'

'You could have waited till I got back. I liked that pic-ture. I wanted to keep it.'

'You never said anything.'

'We never discussed it.'

'Look, we had to make some progress. We have to sell

everything that has any value, otherwise the will won't go to probate before we move out of the house.' Ralph pauses. 'Anyway, I don't think it was very good. I couldn't even tell what it was.'

'It was a man driving a chariot.'

'I couldn't see that. And it was ugly – the colours . . .'

'I thought it was ugly too,' Robin says.

Lead-grey, clotted cream, sand: there was a kind of grace in the way Braque had shunned anything primary or obvious.

'I don't think it was ugly at all,' I say. 'I *liked* it.'

'Well, I *never* liked it,' Ralph says.

'All the more reason for me to have it then.'

Ralph sighs.

'I mean, it was a *Braque*,' I say.

Ralph leans over the table, hands clasped in front of him, and I see a side of him I haven't seen before. He has a ruthless streak; he can be unwavering, dismissive. Suddenly I can imagine him in a boardroom, closing a deal. The hands calm and resolute, the faint curl of the upper lip. The occasional cunning sideways glance . . . Is he relishing the fact that he has outmanoeuvred me? Or is he merely thinking I have brought this on myself? Because he's right. I have. Robin and I have been quite content to let Ralph assume responsibility for the probate. It's Ralph who has been doing all the work.

'You can't have been *that* bothered about it,' he says, 'or you wouldn't have gone away for so long.'

A spark of anger glows, and is then extinguished. Do I *really* want the lithograph? If so, why not drive down to Edgar Horn? I could find the person in charge and explain that there has been an error. I could talk about a family in mourning, a difficult time, irrational behaviour. I could apologize for the misunderstanding, offer to refund the money. Surely, given the circumstances, they would not object. But even as the idea occurs to me, I know I won't make the slightest effort to retrieve the Braque. What will I do? Nothing. There is a lot, it seems to me, that I'm not doing.

The lithograph has gone, I tell myself. Things of great value are always disappearing, never to be seen again. Things I love. Well, perhaps I'm not supposed to have them. Perhaps I should stop trying to hold on. After all, how much of the past does anybody really need to keep? Though this argument strikes me as perfectly valid, I can't help noticing my anger has flared up again. I wanted the Braque. I *wanted* it.

Later that day, I check my copy of the letter that accompanied Dad's will. Given the care with which he allocated items as mundane as a slide projector or a radio cassette, it seems inconceivable that he could have disregarded the lithograph, but I go through all five pages and fail to find a single reference to it. Was he uncertain about who to leave it to? Or, aware of its worth, was he unwilling to favour one of his children over all the others? I raise the subject with Robin after Ralph and Vivian have gone upstairs to bed. Robin thinks it was an oversight: Dad just forgot.

In that same letter, Dad talked about his pictures. He appeared to accept that we wouldn't be able to keep his entire output – *concerning my paintings, you must do your best to be fair*, he wrote, *but I understand that some will be destroyed* – yet in those measured words I seem to hear a note of disappointment, a thinly concealed plea. He always believed his work had merit, even if the art world and the general public chose to ignore it.

Dad's pictures fall into several categories. In the fifties and sixties he painted female nudes. The hair is always long, straight and dark brown, with a centre parting and a fringe. The breasts are small and round, with a space between them, and the pubic triangle is a neat, inverted pyramid. Now that I look at the pictures again, I see something of Sonya in them, even though Dad had yet to meet her. In the strong, slim body and the shapely legs, there are clear echoes of my mother too. This woman who he returned to again and again must have corresponded to his ideal. I don't remember a single painting of a blonde.

His figurative work includes several landscapes, but most of what he produced was abstract. Typically, the paintings were about six feet long and two or three feet high, and since he couldn't afford canvas, the oils were applied directly on to sheets of hardboard. The slashes and dribbles of colour, which seem lifted straight from Jackson Pollock, were sometimes imprisoned behind a lattice of harsh black lines. Dad made his own frames, using narrow strips of pine, and there would be a small square of white paper on the back of every picture, on which he would write the title, the year and a price. His titles are as abstract as the art – 'Convergence', 'Resolution' – but it is the prices that upset me most. They're so optimistic, so notional; I'm not sure he sold more than one or two pieces of work in his entire life.

In the seventies, he entered what he only half-jokingly called his 'Lines-and-Balls' period. These pictures are smaller, but the titles remain obscure. Every time I arrived back home at the end of term, I would have to go and look at what he had done while I had been away. Positioning myself in front of 'Balance', a large monochrome Lines-and-Balls painting he had hung inside the sitting-room door, I remember tilting my head, as I had seen people do in galleries.

'What do you think?' Dad was behind me, in his red chair, peering over the top of his half-moon spectacles.

'I quite like it.'

'Really?'

I nodded. 'Not bad.'

When I turned to face him, he was smiling.

'Well done,' he said.

He looked proud – not of himself, but of me. Was it because I had seen some value in his work, or because I had been loyal?

Once, in the late sixties, Cyril Connolly came to our house. His daughter had been playing with Ralph that afternoon – they were in the same class at school – and he had dropped in to pick her up. I watched him pause in front of a painting called 'Summer'. With his monumental bald head and his shapeless grey plastic mackintosh, Cyril Connolly seemed to fill the sitting-room, an effect I put down to the fact that he was famous. He spent at least a minute studying the clustered dabs of red and blue while Dad and I hovered anxiously in the background.

'One of yours?' he enquired eventually, and without taking his eyes off the painting.

Dad admitted that it was.

'Charming,' the great man said. 'Quite charming.'

For Dad, as an artist, this was a moment of glory, and he would often refer to it in the years that followed: 'Well, as *Cyril Connolly* once said . . .'

I decide to keep 'Summer', and I also keep two Lines-and-Balls paintings that used to hang in my bedroom, along with a number of Dad's later efforts, which were executed on the back of Christmas cards, or the inside of cereal packets, or on the covers of the annual reports of companies in which he had shares. Once we have made our own selections, we ring all the people who knew Dad, asking them to take as many paintings as they like, but even after everyone has been, dozens of works remain, and we store them upright against the back wall of the main glasshouse, ready for the inevitable fire.

I stand in the glasshouse, going through the stacks of unwanted paintings. What do I think of Dad's work – really? If I set my loyalty aside, I suppose what I see is a lack of authenticity, a failure of nerve. He seemed either unwilling, or unable, to engage with his own intense emotions, but perhaps the events that so utterly derailed his life were too painful for him to contemplate, let alone explore. He could only try and forget. His art, too, was all about looking away.

According to the local paper, the Curzon is showing the film of David Bowie's 1973 concert at the Hammersmith Odeon. I pass the paper to Robin. We reminisce about how we thought of going to that concert, and then decided against it, worried that seeing Bowie on stage might be a let-down. We have regretted the decision ever since, especially as Bowie chose that night to announce – prematurely, as it turned out – that he would never play live again. Robin says the film is supposed to be good, and when the weekend arrives, we equip ourselves with cigarettes and pre-mixed bottles of vodka-and-orange, and drive downtown.

The Curzon has seen better days. The air is motionless and stale, like stored breath, and when I take my seat I can feel springs poking through the bald red plush. The lights dim; I look around. Apart from us, there are only three or four people in the cinema.

The film opens with Bowie sitting in front of a mirror in his dressing-room. As I watch a young woman put his make-up on, I remember how I would buy each new album the moment it came out. At the end of my first year at university, I InterRailed round Europe with *Diamond Dogs* playing in my head, and were it not for *Aladdin Sane* I doubt I would have flown to America after graduating. Bowie wrote the soundtrack for that part of my life. There's something not quite right about the film, though. The picture is fuzzy, the sound muffled. I glance at Robin. He rolls his eyes. We decide to be patient, assuming the management will notice and make adjustments.

Five minutes pass. Bowie takes the stage with a fast, elastic version of 'Hang on to Yourself', but the sound and picture quality are still poor. Turning in my seat, I peer up at the small square window where the projectionist should be.

'This is ridiculous,' Robin says. 'I mean, what's the point?'

I tell him I will go and speak to someone.

I walk back through the curtain. There is no one standing behind the sweets counter, and the ticket booth is empty. A clock ticks above the trays of Opal Fruits and Maltesers. Its black second hand is the only thing in the foyer that is moving, which gives it a sinister quality, an air of menace. I turn slowly, in a half-circle. Beyond the popcorn machine is a man in a dark blue jacket with a long-handled dustpan and brush. Though he is looking straight at me, his eyes are blank as doorknobs. He has a five o'clock shadow that seems oversimplified, comically precise, as if, like a transfer, it came free with a packet of bubblegum and he stuck it on himself.

'The picture's out of focus,' I tell him. 'The sound's bad too. Could you have a word with the projectionist?'

The man's eyes seem to change angle, like blinds, and he stares down at his dustpan. I'm not convinced he will do anything at all, or even that he has understood.

Back in the cinema, I drop into my seat. The camera has turned its gaze on Bowie's audience. Hands lift and sway in the grainy, soot-black air of the Odeon. Such light as there is seems tangerine. The people in the front row are all singing along; they know the words off by heart. The camera homes in. A girl's face shifts almost lazily from left to right. Her mouth opens, and stays open, half in happiness, half in awe; a strand of dark hair sticks to her cheek. We should have gone. We were idiots. I swallow a mouthful of vodka-and-orange, then light a cigarette.

Without taking his eyes off the screen, Robin moves his head towards mine. 'What did they say?'

I tell him about the man with the dustpan and brush. 'I'm not sure it's going to do any good,' I say.

During 'Time', Bowie writhes on the floor of the stage like a cat on heat. Standing over him, Mick Ronson extracts a few tortured notes from his guitar, face framed by swags of dyed blond hair, lips peeling back in a kind of anguish. The picture has improved, but the sound is still dirty and subdued.

'Oh, this is crap,' Robin says. Swivelling in his seat, he yells, 'Turn the volume up.'

Suddenly he seems much drunker than me. I take a long swig from my bottle, then I too shout, 'Turn it up.'

We carry on watching. We want to complain, but at the

same time we don't want to miss anything. The spotlight discovers Bowie on a stool with a twelve-string guitar. The camera moves closer. Looks up from below. Bowie's face is frost-blue, and the whites of his eyes, as he gazes out into the dark, are spotless.

'My death waits . . .' he sings.

'I *love* this song.' Robin lurches round in his seat again. 'We can't hear it,' he bellows. 'Turn it up!'

I join in.

Sometimes the other members of the audience look at us – I can see the pale discs of their faces – and I know they're frustrated too, and that they would also be protesting if only they'd had a bit of vodka.

The sound level drops.

'We might as well be in the foyer,' I tell Robin.

'Or out on the fucking street,' he says.

Robin stands, all six foot three of him. Facing the back of the cinema, he puts his hands on either side of his mouth to form a sort of megaphone.

'TURN THE VOLUME UP!'

When he takes his seat again, he looks pleased with himself, as if he thinks this might have done the trick.

Thirty seconds pass. Nothing changes. Then, purely by chance, we both start shouting at the same time.

'TURN – IT – UP!'

After the first encore, 'White Light, White Heat', Bowie tells the audience that of all the shows they have done, this one will remain with him the longest, not just because it's the last show of the tour but because it's the last show they will ever do, and we would like to be able to savour the gasps of dismay and disbelief that follow this shock announcement, but none of it is audible.

The second encore is 'Rock 'n' Roll Suicide', Bowie's

classic closing number. *Give me your hands ... You're wonderful ...* Robin and I drain our bottles of vodka-and-orange, then stub out our cigarettes.

The credits roll.

Still sitting in our seats, we both undo our flies.

Two streams of urine rush down the slope and pool in the flat area below the screen.

Last Nights

It's four-thirty in the morning, and I have just finished work. Before I go to bed, I begin another letter to Hanne. *I seem to be worried all the time*, I tell her. *The thought of the future fills me with panic*. I cross out *fills me with panic*. The thought of the future – what? I stare straight ahead, the garden invisible below.

Since midnight, the wind has strengthened, and the doors and windows are rattling. It doesn't feel like August. Bending over my letter, I tell Hanne about Rosie and Hal, who have been staying with us. When they walked out of Arrivals, clutching their little suitcases, they had name tags dangling round their necks, and I couldn't help but see them, just for a moment, as refugees. Their quietness unnerved me. We drove south, back to the house, trees as black as burnt paper against a clear blue evening sky. I caught a glimpse of Rosie in the rear-view mirror, her face close to the window. She broke a long silence by talking about the road, and how she remembered it from all the other times. Dad would always come for them, she said. She called him Dad, just as we did.

Their holiday coincided with the Los Angeles Olympics, and they installed themselves on Dad's bed with the curtains drawn and the TV on, their backs against the headboard and their legs stretched out in front of them. I remember peering into the flickering gloom and asking if they were all right. Oh yes, Rosie said. We're fine. It's sunny, I said. Don't you want to play outside? Though Rosie's eyes didn't leave the screen, she appeared to give my idea some thought. Maybe later, she said eventually. I sensed that the real answer to my question was, not really, but that she was trying not to hurt my feelings.

When they weren't watching the Olympics, they would wander from room to room, pointing at objects and ornaments. That's mine, isn't it? they'd say. Or, Dad promised to give me that. They often asked about money – how much would they be getting? – and they were curious about the house, wanting to know who owned it, and what it was worth. *It can't be normal, can it*, I write to Hanne, *for children to be preoccupied with such things?* There were times when Robin and I thought we could hear learned lines – a voice in the background, coaching them. It seemed the only possible explanation. We already knew Sonya didn't trust us. Why else would she have hired a lawyer? One morning in the second week, Rosie once again brought up the subject of the will, and Vivian turned on her and snapped, Stop asking about money, will you? I'm fed up with it. Rosie burst into tears. I don't want to ask all these questions, she said, and Robin and I exchanged a glance, for here, surely, was something that appeared to confirm our suspicions.

I tell Hanne how we lit a bonfire on one of the last nights, thinking we could have a picnic under the stars. As I walked back to the house to collect potatoes and silver

foil, Rosie's face floated through the darkness towards me.
She asked if she and Hal were staying up. Of course, I
said. Her eyes drifted away from me, across the garden.
We want you to say no, she said. I laughed. You want us to
say no? She nodded gravely. Maybe they wished life were
more like it had been when they stayed with Dad.
Methodical, unvarying. Calm. In filling their holiday with
spontaneity and excess, we had been thinking of ourselves,
perhaps, and what we had missed in our own childhood.
We had been insensitive. Naive. Still, when they went to
bed, we never forgot to kiss them good night and tell them
we loved them, and Rosie's voice always followed us out
of the room with the same quaint, sing-song words: *Thank
you for all the things.*

We organized all kinds of expeditions – the woods, the
pier, the zoo, the beach – but the image that stays with me
is of two children sitting side by side in the nervy black-
and-silver light of the TV. They watched with such
determination. They seemed so small, so lost. They looked
oddly valiant. How did it feel to be back in the house
where they began their lives? Did they miss their father?
What could we do to make them happy? Difficult questions – and even if I were to have asked, I suspect Rosie
would have tried to reassure me. *We're fine. Really.* In her
sublimation of her own feelings, in her transparent diplo-
macy, she often reminded me of myself.

I look up from the page. Outside, it's still dark, and the
rain is coming down in sheets. I tell Hanne about the
yellow patches that have appeared on the back lawn,
marking the places where stepping-stones used to be
during my grandparents' time. I talk about the wallpaper
in my bedroom, which has loosened to reveal elegant pink-
and-gold stripes underneath. It's as though the house is

reminding us of its previous lives, its former glories. *This is what you've turned your back on.* I describe a dream I had, and a shiver zigzags through me as I write. I was standing in the hall, and the house was talking to me, asking me to stay. Though I explained the situation, the house didn't seem to understand. Don't leave me, it kept saying. Don't go.

I tried to reason with the house. We've got no choice, I told it. We can't *afford* to stay. Its voice became louder, and more desperate. Please don't leave. I'm begging you.

We have to, I said.

The house lost its temper. You don't, it shouted. You don't *have* to. I don't *want* you to.

I had goose-bumps now. Nothing I could say would make the slightest difference. The house began to scream, its voice malevolent and guttural. I covered my ears.

YOU CAN'T LEAVE.

I WON'T LET YOU.

DON'T.

FUCKING.

GO.

I still had my hands over my ears, but I was kneeling on the hall floor, my forehead pressed into the carpet. The house was swearing at me. Calling me names. The worst things it could think of.

I look out over the garden, which is surfacing at last like the deck of a sunk ship raised from the deep. *The thought of the future.* I can't even control the present.

It was the radiogram that started it.

For months now, we have known that we need to empty the house, but there are still tables and chairs in every

room. We have contacted all the antiques dealers in town,
and all the charity and junk shops. We must have had half
a dozen garage sales. We have talked to friends, to neighbours – to complete strangers. None of them has any use
for second-hand furniture. We can't even give it away.

One Saturday, after Vivian has taken Greta up to bed,
we sit in the kitchen, drinking. We have decided to go
through Dad's collection of LPs to see if he has anything
worth keeping. We begin with a fifties' musical called *Gigi*,
which stars Maurice Chevalier. The songs are famous –
'Thank Heaven for Little Girls', 'I Remember It Well' – but
one side is enough. Next we put on *Françoise Hardy Sings
about Love*. Ralph has stayed downstairs, and his presence, which is rare these days, seems to have created an air
of expectancy.

As Robin turns the Françoise Hardy record over, he
leans on the radiogram, and one of the front legs gives
slightly. He looks at us across his shoulder. We're all
having the same thought. Ralph tugs at the leg, which
comes away quite easily, and the radiogram sinks to its
knees like a buffalo that has just been shot. Wrenching
the turntable free of its wooden casing, Robin carries it out
to the pile of scrap metal by the garage. There's a silence,
then a decisive crash. He reappears in the kitchen doorway, dusting his hands off on his trousers.

Our eyes sweep round the room. We're not in any doubt
about what needs doing. We make for the scullery, where
Dad keeps all his tools. The cupboard is dark and cool,
and smells of turpentine. Robin selects a short-handled
axe and then steps back. Ralph lifts a saw down off the
wall. I reach for the claw hammer. We return to the
kitchen. Before we begin, Robin rigs up his stereo and puts
on another of Dad's LPs, *Grand Prix*, which is a recording

of Formula One racing cars in action, with live commentaries by John Bolster and Nevil Lloyd. We set to work dismembering the furniture. The chopping and hacking is so loud that we have to turn the volume up. It's Spa, in Belgium, 1958. One by one, the cars snarl by. Lotus, Vanwall. BRM. Though Bolster never loses his composure, his voice has a steely edge, I notice, a kind of whine, as if it, too, is the result of precision engineering. Every now and then, we stop for a glass of cider or a smoke. This is hard work, but in the morning we'll be glad we did it.

When we have finished with the radiogram, the kitchen table and the chairs, we fetch furniture from the study and the sitting-room. John Bolster is about as excited as he will ever get. *Here come the cars ... all going magnificently ...* Swinging with a little too much vigour, Robin misses a table leg, and his axe bites hungrily into the floor. When he frees the axe, which takes all his strength, it leaves a deep indent in the parquet. Looks like a cunt, Ralph says. We know what he means. Worried about how the new owners of the property might react, we decide to pretend that the cunt was there all along. Oh yes, we say, practising. For years. Ever since we were tiny. The air smells of sawdust and cigarettes, and in the brief silence between tracks I can hear a steady buzz, as if we're standing under an electric pylon.

It's midnight when I next look up. The rubble's a foot deep, and there's red stuff on the fridge. I wonder if it's blood. My breath rasps in and out. Overhead, a naked bulb sways on its flex, and all the shadows lurch.

Ralph sprawls face down, his head wedged behind the scullery door. He has passed out on a heap of splintered wood.

I bend over him. 'Ralph? Are you all right?'

His lips move, but I can't understand what he is saying. Still, at least he isn't dead.

Where's Robin, though?

As I try and piece things together, a howl comes from another part of the house. I can't be sure, but I don't think it's the baby. Crossing the hall, I enter the sitting-room. In the glasshouse Robin is standing, legs apart, in front of a squat upholstered chair, the short-handled axe raised high above his head. I pause in the doorway.

'I've always hated this chair,' he says.

He brings the axe down on one of the arms. Woodchips dart through the air. The arm holds firm.

'Fuck.' He drains his glass of cider.

With its low centre of gravity and its short, almost toad-like legs, the chair has a decidedly stubborn look.

Robin lifts the axe again. 'Die!' he yells. The curved blade descends, the black sky ripping open to reveal silver. The chair's arm splits, but doesn't yield.

As Robin prepares to deliver yet another savage blow, a movement distracts me. I look beyond him, to where the light spilling from the house is swallowed by the darkness of the garden. Someone is standing on the lawn, over by the garage. I move closer to Robin and rest a hand on his shoulder.

'Robin,' I say, 'we're not alone.'

As Robin turns, his axe still raised, a figure steps forward into the light. He's wearing a dark uniform with shiny buttons.

'This party's got to stop,' he says.

I stifle a laugh. 'This isn't a *party*,' I tell him. 'It's just the family. We *live* here.'

'There have been complaints . . .'

'Complaints?'

'We've had a number of phone calls,' the policeman says, 'about the noise.' His face is pale and narrow, with a pinched mouth, and I wonder, fleetingly, if he was ever bullied at school.

He glances towards the kitchen. A loud *tsk-tsk-tsk* is coming from the open window. The needle must have reached the end of the record and failed to reject.

'We'll be quiet now,' I say.

'You do that.' The policeman backs away and disappears through the garden gate.

'He was young for a policeman,' Robin says.

'Yes, he was.'

'He seemed nervous.'

I look at Robin. 'Can you blame him?'

Robin lowers his axe.

A few days later, a man with steel-rimmed glasses knocks on our front door. He tells me that he's from the council. When I ask him if he has come about the rubbish, he blinks, then hands me a sheet of paper. 'I'm serving you with a writ,' he says, 'for noise pollution.'

Noise pollution. Now there's an interesting combination of words. I remember Robin's howl as he laid into the toad-like chair. It's a wonder we still have all our fingers.

But the man from the council is turning away.

I follow him as far as the gate. 'What am I supposed to do with this?' I call out, waving the writ.

He doesn't answer, or even glance over his shoulder. The tails of his grey suit jacket flutter anxiously around his buttocks as he hurries off up the road.

*

One night, when Ralph and Vivian are asleep, I slide the drawer out of the trolley that stands next to Dad's bed. Putting Dad's washable Lion Brand condom to one side – a family heirloom, this – I empty every plastic bottle, metallic tube and blister pack that I can find. Throughout our childhood – throughout our lives – Dad would eat his meals quickly, often leaving the table before we had finished. I've got to take my pills, he would say. Curious as to what they do, Robin and I have decided to sample a few of Dad's pills ourselves.

We start with some capsules that are half-red, half-black. Rounded at both ends, they look like miniature warheads. We swallow one each. Lying back on the bed, I wonder idly whose job it is to decide what colour pills are going to be. Are there special people?

Dad's TV is on. We watch part of a comedy programme, but the canned laughter gets on our nerves, and we switch channels.

We wait about ten minutes, then take a couple of grey-green pills – Euhypnos 40 – which we follow with a vicious-looking red-and-white capsule that makes me think of toadstools. As I rest my head against a stack of Dad's pillows, I notice they no longer smell of him.

'The news is soon,' Robin says. 'You want to watch the news?'

I haven't seen the news in months.

'How do you feel?' I ask him.

'All right. A bit floaty.' He points. 'What are those round ones?'

'These?' I hold up a glowing, light brown pill that seems to be filled with liquid. 'Fish-oil, I think. They're supposed to be good for you.'

'Don't need those, then.'

I smile.

We watch more television – a programme about fast cars. Some time later, I ask Robin if we have tried the yellow pills.

'I don't think so,' he says.

It occurs to me that one of us ought to have been keeping track of what we've taken.

I pass him a yellow pill and swallow one myself, then I lie back again. My eyes drift from the TV to the psychedelic curtains. Though they're blue – Dad's favourite colour – I can't imagine that he chose them. They must have been Sonya's idea. I seem to catch a glimpse of her, no clothes on, her breasts a startled white.

Quickly, I turn back to Robin. 'How are you feeling?'

'You already asked me that,' he says.

'That was ages ago.'

'Really?' He reaches for his glass of water. 'I don't feel too bad, actually. Mouth's a bit dry.'

'They don't seem to be doing much.'

'Maybe they're stale.'

'Is there a date on them?'

Robin studies the label on the bottle nearest to him. 'This one says 1982.'

Changing channels again, he finds a programme about the miners' strike. Industrial action has been going on for most of the year, but it hasn't affected us too much down south. While in London, though, we saw men with plastic buckets in the entrances to tube stations, collecting money for the miners' families, and in Stanley people talked of nothing else.

We watch footage of the picket lines. Men with clenched fists. Home-made banners. Mounted police. The horses seem enormous, eyes flaring behind their blinkers.

'How many have we had, do you think?' Robin says.

'What, altogether?'

He nods.

'I don't know. Fifteen?'

'What if one of us passes out?'

I think for a moment. 'I suppose the other one will have to call an ambulance.'

'What if we both pass out?'

'They'll find us in the morning. It'll be like one of those suicide pacts.'

'No note, though.'

'You think we should write something,' I say, 'just in case?'

Robin appears to consider this.

'I can't be bothered,' he says at last.

'Nor can I,' I say.

Arthur Scargill is haranguing a crowd from the back of a lorry. We approve of Scargill, with his bluntness and his passion and his hair that looks like a rusty Brillo pad. We approve of anyone who stands up to Maggie Thatcher.

I reach for an empty pill box. Dad's name is written on the label in blue biro. 'Do you miss him?' I say.

'Who, Dad?'

I nod.

'Yes,' Robin says. 'I suppose so.'

'I got so used to him being here. I sort of thought he would be here for ever.'

Robin watches me sidelong.

'He used to say, If something happens to me,' I go on, 'and for years nothing did.'

A map of the British Isles appears on TV. The weatherman moves his hand in smooth, repeated arcs, as if polishing the windscreen of a car.

'He'd always say, If something happens to me. He never said, If I die . . .'

Midway through the forecast, the weatherman is replaced by Dad. At the beginning of the school holidays, Dad would usually sit me down and ask if I would like to hear one or two of his longer poems. It was a joke, a routine, and I would groan or roll my eyes, but I knew that, under all the clowning, he was desperate to read to me. He has the same expression now: self-deprecating, hopeful. He is wearing faded maroon trousers, a striped shirt and a dark blue zip-up cardigan, and though his feet are out of shot, I know he has his slippers on, the ones with bits of carpet glued to the soles. When Dad predicts a gale-force wind, he grins self-consciously. In our family, the word 'wind' was often used instead of 'fart', and Dad has just made the connection. *Don't*, I can almost hear him saying. *Don't make me laugh.*

'I'm sorry he died all alone, with none of us there,' I say. 'I think about that.'

I stare out across the room, towards the fireplace. The air seems to have swollen; it looks elongated, somehow, and slightly grey. I have a sense of having to peer through it, like a mist, to see the wall.

'I can't cry about him yet,' I say, 'not properly. I don't know why. I just can't.'

'I haven't cried yet either,' Robin says.

'You were sick, though.'

'That's true.'

I haven't even begun to grieve. It's the same as twenty years ago. Like water through limestone, this new sorrow is following the path formed by the old one, both sorrows hidden, buried, unexpressed.

I wake up wearing all my clothes. Robin is asleep beside

me. The lights are still on. So is the TV, its blank screen hissing. I turn the TV off, then put my ear close to Robin's mouth. His breath smells of plastic, but his breathing sounds regular enough.

We haven't written our suicide note. Oh well.

It's all I can do to remove my shirt and trousers, switch off the light and climb under the covers.

I'm asleep again in seconds.

Moonlight Represents My Heart

I set off for Shanghai on a Saturday in December 2007. The Piccadilly Line was crowded with men in blue football shirts – Chelsea had played at home that afternoon – and somewhere after Hammersmith a woman standing near me crumpled and slid down the door. Her black cloche hat toppled off her head, and the lacquered red leather purse she was holding slipped out of her hands and landed on the floor at my feet. The man travelling with her laid his suitcase flat, lowered her on to it, and then stooped over her, carefully brushing her tawny hair back off her forehead. They were German; I had heard them talking earlier, as I stepped on to the train.

When the woman came round, she murmured that she needed air. A fellow passenger opened the narrow window at our end of the carriage. The woman's head lifted. 'Thank you,' she said. 'Thank you so much.' On her left hand were several ornate gold rings. She glanced up, her eyes finding mine, and gave me one of the most radiant smiles I had ever seen. Though she was probably in her late fifties, she looked, for a moment, like a young girl, and

I wondered if the radiance was linked to her momentary loss of consciousness, or if, like her tawny hair, it was part of who she was. I asked her whether she felt better, and she nodded and waved a hand in front of her face. I passed her the hat, which she placed on her head, then I handed her the purse. She smiled at me again, her eyes wide and preternaturally bright. 'Thank you. You're very kind.' I told her that when she stood up she should do it slowly. The blood needed time to reach the brain. 'I know about it,' I said. 'I used to faint a lot when I was young.' The man leaned towards her. 'He is paying you a compliment,' he said. Now all three of us were smiling.

I landed in Paris half an hour behind schedule and had to run through Charles de Gaulle to catch my connecting flight. Once airborne for the second time, I asked for wine and watched the new film by Chabrol. Every now and then, I thought of the German couple. I had seen them in Departures at Heathrow, sitting side by side on plastic chairs. To live close to that smile – within its range, as it were – would be like living in a kind of sunlight. You'd feel blessed. Just before I slept, I peered out of the window: a wide, thin shelf of cloud, and the lights of St Petersburg beyond . . .

It was dark again by the time we landed in Pudong. When my suitcase failed to appear on the carousel, an official directed me to Baggage Claim, where an Englishman in a crumpled linen suit was complaining about his own lost luggage. His outrage seemed to be having some effect, and I moved closer to him, hoping to be carried along in the slipstream.

Later, we shared a taxi, and it emerged, in conversation, that he was the father of a friend of mine, and that I had met him before, eighteen years ago, at her wedding. He had also read my latest book, which she had given him for his last birthday. Though happy to see him, and entertained by these elaborate layers of coincidence, I kept my eyes on the window, keen to soak up every detail of our drive into Shanghai. The swooping concrete flyovers, the burnt, brown light collecting round the street lamps; the clinging, almost sticky mist. My stomach tightened. I wasn't just arriving in a new city. Tomorrow I would be having lunch with Ralph, who I hadn't seen for twenty-three years.

That night, in my hotel in the French Concession, I drifted off to sleep at about one-thirty, only to wake again at six. The incident on the tube kept repeating behind my closed eyelids, and in an increasingly lurid and distorted form. The German woman was smiling at me from the floor of the train – *You're kind, so kind* – but her hair stuck to her forehead in sweat-darkened spikes, and her purse, which was the colour of a wound, lay at a queasy angle to my shoe. In my anxious, jet-lagged state, her eyes seemed like the eyes of someone suffering from malnutrition, and her smile was no longer a blessing but an admission of weakness, a bright flash of fear. At the same time, I was tormented by the fact of my missing luggage. I wouldn't be able to give Ralph the presents I had bought for him, and I would have to meet him wearing dirty clothes. I would be empty-handed, unclean. Disreputable. Only half awake, I shifted in the bed, seeking respite from this torrent of unwanted images and thoughts.

At last I could make out the gaps between the blinds, and I got up and walked to the window. A steady rain was falling; distant apartment blocks showed as blurred grey oblongs. On the street below, the cyclists wore brightly coloured plastic ponchos that covered not only their shoulders but the handlebars and saddles of their bicycles as well. I showered, then put on the clothes I had worn on the plane and took a lift up to the eleventh floor for breakfast.

At half past nine I dialled the work number Ralph had given me. He answered after just three rings.

'You're here, then,' he said.

It was twenty years since we had spoken to each other. My mind folded shut, and I had no idea what to say.

He asked whether I still felt like having lunch. If so, it might be best if I came to the bank. We could eat somewhere nearby. 'We'll start respectably,' he said, 'and go downhill from there.' We could also meet that evening, though he couldn't stay out late.

'I'd love to,' I said.

I hoped I hadn't sounded too eager. Though I had told him I had always wanted to visit Shanghai, I doubted I would have come had he not been living there, and yet if he felt I'd travelled all this way just to see him, it might frighten him off. Even now, he could say that he'd had second thoughts. He could cancel, or simply not turn up.

I left my hotel at about eleven. Outside, it was murky, but at least the rain had stopped. The air smelled of stale gingerbread, and also, faintly, of sulphur. I found myself on a busy shopping street called Huaihai Lu. From hidden speakers came the bright, breathy, tinny voice of a young woman. She might have been advertising a special one-off Christmas promotion, but the halo of reverb that shimmered around everything she said, and the Chinese itself, with its abrupt rising and dipping tones, made her sound eerie, and utterly alien. I thought of evil spells, unquiet souls. I thought of sirens. How had it felt to hear Ralph's voice on the phone? I had known it was him, of course, but had it *sounded* like him? Oddly enough, when he first started talking, he had reminded me of Uncle Roland, even

though I hadn't spoken to Uncle Roland since Dad's
funeral. In the end, it wasn't Ralph's voice I had recognized, but something *beneath* his voice: a shared history,
perhaps, or even a way of seeing things, a way of being. *I
know who you are and you know who I am*. We were
strangers, in other words, but only on the surface.

I flagged down a taxi and handed the driver a piece of
paper Ralph had left at my hotel. It was the address of his
office, written in Chinese. Twenty minutes later, the taxi
stopped outside a building in Pudong. The lobby
gleamed, its corners restless with TV screens. I took a lift
to the tenth floor. The bank's glass doors were locked.
I pressed the buzzer, and a young Chinese man let me in. I
told him who I had come to see. He asked for my business
card. 'I'm his brother,' I said. He laughed, then led me
across an open-plan area and motioned to a door that
stood ajar.

When I stepped into Ralph's office, which was small
and unpretentious, no more than fifteen feet by eight, he
was sitting sideways-on to me, in a black swivel chair. He
was on the phone, speaking Italian. '*Sempre così. Sì, sì.
Lo so*.' Looking up, he smiled and waved me to the only
other chair. As I took a seat, I suddenly regretted having
seen Uncle Frank's photos. Since I had known what
Ralph would look like, his physical appearance hadn't
had the impact it might otherwise have done. Perhaps
for that reason, I scrutinized his clothes. He was wearing
a run-of-the-mill grey suit, a white shirt that didn't seem
particularly new, and a generic dark blue tie. Somehow, I
had expected him to be smarter, sleeker – more corporate.
I found myself staring at his hands, which were bigger
than I remembered, with fingers that looked muscular.
Behind him, in the window, I could see the business

district, all science-fiction high-rise towers and multi-lane main roads. The air was the colour of raw onion.

The phone call over, Ralph rose from his chair. 'Sorry about that.' He walked round the desk, and we gave each other a hug. I felt a brief shudder, as though we had been caught in a minor earthquake. I couldn't tell where it had come from – him, or me, or both of us.

'So this is where you work,' I said.

Shrugging, Ralph glanced around. He didn't really think of himself as a banker, he said. He was more like a musician who happened to have a job in a bank. I asked about his music. He still played the trumpet, he told me – during his first year in China he had been in a band, jazz and blues mostly – and he was also learning the guitar. He often sang in karaoke places. The Chinese were mad about karaoke.

I passed Ralph photographs of Kate and Evie, and as he looked at them I suddenly saw them as proof of something, like a reference or an affidavit, like a badge. It seemed important that he should look at them and know who I had become. He needed to understand that I had done as he had done. We both had people we lived for, people whose lives we would defend with our own. I told him I had spoken to Sonya recently, for the first time in years, and that it had shocked her to learn that I had a wife and daughter. She had assumed I would always be alone, describing me as 'a little bit separated'. Ralph chose not to comment. Instead, he opened a file in his computer and showed me some pictures of his own family. There was a photo of his sons, both adults now. They looked rugged, confident, reminding me of the kind of French actors who played gangsters in the fifties and sixties.

On our way to lunch, Ralph kept snatching glances at me, and I thought I saw amusement on his face, and disbelief, that I had flown to China, as I had said I would, that we were together after all these years, that this was actually happening, and once, as we crossed a featureless piazza, he reached out quickly and skimmed a hand over the top of my head. 'Look at that lovely hair,' he said.

We took an escalator to the first floor of a neighbouring high-rise. The restaurant Ralph had chosen, Wang Chao, was enormous and grandiose, with black-and-gilt urns on pedestals and paté-coloured marble walls. Since the menus were in Chinese, I left the ordering to Ralph. Large bottles of beer appeared. The skin above and below my eyes felt stiff, and my thoughts wobbled and lurched like one of Dad's Super 8 home movies. For me, it was five o'clock in the morning.

I told Ralph about my missing suitcase. The same thing had happened to him, he said, when he first arrived. Three days later, the luggage was delivered to his house. He told me not to worry. I felt he thought I was being unnecessarily fretful. I also sensed that material possessions meant little or nothing to him. He didn't care what kind of suit he wore, or how his office looked. Luggage? That didn't matter. *This* mattered. Being out. Talking. He was flipping through the menu – forwards, backwards, forwards again. Even sitting down, he exuded energy and self-assurance. He had an exchange with the waiter, who backed away with an uncertain smile.

'They don't like it if you make jokes in restaurants,' Ralph told me. 'They get confused.' He shook his head. 'Sometimes I really hate the Chinese – all one point seven billion of them.' Grinning, he reached for his beer.

We drank fast and chain-smoked cigarettes called

Shanghai Gold. Our conversation jumped from subject to subject, often halfway through a sentence. I had so many questions for Ralph, but at the same time I was content simply to be with him, having lunch. In retrospect, I was glad he had asked me not to record him. Truman Capote once said that a tape recorder destroys any naturalness that might exist between what he referred to as 'the nervous humming-bird and its would-be captor', and this naturalness, I felt, was the very state that we were trying to recapture or achieve.

The food began to arrive – a tureen of sour hot soup, and crab-meat tofu in a terracotta bowl. I asked Ralph about the eggs, which were a peculiar bruised blue-green.

'*Pidan doufu,*' he said. 'Hundred-year-old eggs. They're not a hundred years old, of course.' He selected one with his chopsticks and ate it, then made a face. 'Horrible.'

Now I was grinning. 'Good colour, though.'

'I only got them for the colour. You don't have to eat them.'

Something hallucinogenic was happening: whenever I took my eyes off Ralph, I found that I couldn't remember what he looked like, and even if I stared at him, his face would alter, reverting to how it had been when he was nine or ten, a time when I had known him well, or else, and more disturbingly, transforming itself into the face of a friend of mine from New Zealand whom Ralph now happened to resemble. I tried to home in on certain specific features – the creases on his forehead, the deep-set eyes, the humorous mouth – but my brain seemed reluctant to retain or even to process the updated image.

He gave me another of his rapid sidelong glances. 'This is all right. This is fine.' He nodded. 'Well done.'

I smiled. He was using one of Dad's catchphrases.

'Really,' Ralph said. 'I'm glad you came. I'm glad you got in touch. I'm not sure I ever would have.'

We raised our glasses and drank. He would take me for a stroll that evening, he said, signalling for more beer. In a recent e-mail, I had mentioned a liking for dilapidation, and he had discovered an area he thought might interest me.

'I have some questions about 1984,' I said. 'Quite a lot of questions, actually. I don't want to start just yet, though. Maybe tonight.'

'You can ask me anything you like,' he said, 'but I warn you: I'll be brutally frank.'

'Good. There's no point otherwise.'

He told me he had put some thoughts down on paper only weeks after leaving the house, when everything was still fresh in his memory. He said that what he'd written was really vicious. I nodded. The past was so long ago that we seemed to be talking about entirely different people, and I thought this sense of disconnection would make it difficult for either of us to take offence at anything that might be said.

At six o'clock that evening I found myself in another taxi, racing up a slip road on to the elevated highway that roller-coastered across the city, east to west. The concrete walls enclosing us glowed with a supernatural lime-green light. As we joined the flow of traffic, tall buildings massed on either side, one topped with steel horns, another with a crown, a third with what looked like a monumental steer-ing wheel. They, too, were doused in exotic shades of neon – acid yellow, turquoise, damson – and many of the façades doubled as screens that showed commercials. The excitement I felt reminded me of trips to New York when

I was in my early twenties, my eyes pinned wide, my heart fizzing, threatening to vaporize.

When I arrived in Ralph's office for the second time that day, he had already changed into what he called 'plain clothes' – a dark, chunky roll-neck sweater, black trousers, and black shoes. He muttered to himself as he lunged and darted round the office. 'What do I need? Keys, money, lighter . . . Cigarettes! Where are my cigarettes?' As at lunchtime, I was struck by his unusual vitality: it was almost visible, like shock waves, or an aura. I watched him pull on a long black raincoat that was cut like an Australian duster, then we left the bank by a side door and took the lift down to street level.

Our taxi driver, who was young, with wispy hair and nicotine-stained teeth, kept looking round at us as he drove. He and Ralph were having a detailed discussion about the route.

At last, Ralph leaned back. 'They find it difficult if you don't give them a proper destination,' he said. 'Where we're going, it's just a certain point on a road – there's no address – and he can't get his head around it.'

We were in the shadow of a flyover whose stanchions were so tall that the road above us seemed to totter, like somebody on stilts. If I looked behind me, Ralph said, I would see the Yangpu bridge – 'the big bridge', as the Chinese called it – but when I turned in the seat the window was steamed up.

'It smells in here,' I said. 'Of feet.'

Ralph nodded. 'Taxi drivers often sleep in their cars.'

To our right, and ghostly in the gloom, were dozens of blocks of flats, none less than twenty storeys high. They looked anonymous, forbidding, and fertile, somehow, as if they might be capable of self-replicating.

Ralph gestured at our driver. 'Do you want to ask him something?'

'Has he got a girlfriend?'

Ralph put the question for me, and the driver replied.

'He's got a wife,' Ralph said.

'Is she beautiful?' I asked.

The answer came back.

'She's average,' Ralph said.

We both laughed.

'You see, I like that,' Ralph said. 'The Chinese are so matter-of-fact. They see things exactly as they are.'

The taxi stopped, and I got out. The road, which was wide and straight, seemed to disappear into nothingness. Out there somewhere was Changxing Island and the East China Sea. A dense mist closed around the street lamps, stifling the light they gave off. There were no houses, and no cars. Very seldom in my life had I felt so far away from everything.

We crossed a rough grass verge, then climbed through a gap in a low wall. I found myself standing on a muddy, unpaved track. The rain was holding off; the damp air swirled. Up ahead, I could make out the dim outlines of buildings. Were they still under construction, or already derelict? I couldn't tell. Shadowy figures moved through unfurnished rooms, a woman's lowered forehead coaxed into existence by a kerosene lamp, a man's hand floating in a pool of light. Windows with no glass in them. Doorways, but no doors. Off to the right, a Buddhist temple stood on its own in the shattered landscape, surprisingly whole and perfect, like the sole survivor of a heavy bombing-raid. I felt we had wandered into a war zone.

We turned left into a paved alley. It was suppertime, and most people were busy cooking. Noodles whirled in dented vats. Clouds of steam poured from under slack tarpaulins. All the smells were water-related: boiled vegetables, damp washing, mould. Ralph said the inhabitants were from the Anhui province, which was north-west of Shanghai, in central China. They had come to the city to work on the building sites.

Further up the alley, we bought bottles of beer and played pool beneath a slanting sheet of corrugated plastic. Hurricane lamps hung from rusty hooks above our heads, and fifteen or twenty scruffy-looking men watched intently from the shadows, their arms folded. The surface of the table was so warped that if you hit a ball too softly it would curve away from the pocket. Everything was moist; my cue kept sticking to the web of skin between my thumb and my forefinger. Sometimes we had to straddle puddles to play our shots. There was a strong smell of urine. In China, Ralph told me, you could piss anywhere you liked.

'I'm playing pool outside,' I said, 'in December –'

'In Shanghai,' Ralph said.

But I had been about to say, With you.

After he had beaten me two games to one, we moved on up the street, taking our beers with us.

Ten minutes later, we came out on to a main road. Broken kerbstones, a shop selling exhaust pipes and electric fans. Street lights like a row of dirty yellow peonies.

'Ask me a question,' Ralph said.

'All right. It's big, though.'

He nodded. 'OK.'

'What was I like?'

'What were you like?' He stared straight ahead, into the mist. 'That's a good one.'

We took a right turn along a desolate canal.

'You were wearing black probably,' he said, 'when you arrived. In those days you always wore black.' He paused. 'You were very close to Robin. You seemed obsessed with him.'

'Obsessed?'

'There was this whole thing of sleeping together – in Goat's bed.'

I couldn't help grinning. I had forgotten that we used to call Dad 'Goat'. Obviously Ralph and Vivian still did.

'I don't know who slept in that room first,' Ralph went on.

'Robin did.'

'But you chose to sleep in the same bed . . .'

'I suppose it was the only bed that was made up when I arrived.'

Ralph gave me a look I couldn't interpret.

'How long did I sleep in Dad's room anyway?' I asked.

'About a month.'

'I thought it was only until after the funeral.'

Ralph shrugged. 'That's what I remember.'

The canal lay to my left, smooth and grey as sheet metal, the far bank fringed with coarse pale yellow grasses. To our right stood a row of concrete houses. Fluorescent strip lights filled each interior with a bleak white glare. In rooms that looked over-exposed, people were preparing food, mending clothes. Playing mah-jongg.

'We thought you were having a sexual relationship,' Ralph said.

I stared at him.

'We didn't judge,' he said. 'You know, we thought, Well, if that's what's going on, that's cool.'

'You thought we were having sex?'

'Yes.' He looked at me. 'Weren't you?'

'No.' My voice bounced off the flat surface of the canal. I had spoken more loudly than I'd meant to.

'You were always together,' Ralph went on. 'Robin was the more dominant one – no, that's putting it too strongly . . .'

'So was I – I don't know – submissive?'

'Not exactly. You just wanted to be with him all the time.' Ralph stared at the ground. 'You were infatuated.'

We had reached a junction. On the roof of a nearby lean-to was a crooked stovepipe, and orange sparks seemed flung, crackling, into the misty air. Two women stood in a doorway below, their backs to us, tending to a wood fire. Like everybody else, they were hard at work on their evening meal.

Startled by Ralph's answer to my first question, and unsure where to go with it, I jumped straight to the next one. What had been the cause of our original estrangement in 1980? Had I said or done something, or was it Tina?

He gave me a sideways look. 'You don't remember?'

I shook my head.

'It was Tina,' he said. 'She said she really wanted to paint Vivian because it was always much more interesting to paint people who weren't beautiful.'

'She said *that*?'

'Vivian thought, Fuck you. She didn't want to have anything to do with Tina after that.'

I suspected Tina had said – or meant to say – that she liked painting people who weren't *obviously* beautiful – coming from Tina, this would have been a compliment; it was the way she saw herself – but there was little point in trying to explain this to Ralph twenty-seven years later.

'So that was why you stopped seeing us?' I said.

He nodded. 'Yes.'

'And then I refused to be your best man. That must have made things worse . . .'

'I suppose it was a bit of a blow. But, you know – blokes: we get over things like that. Women are different.' Ralph allowed himself a crumpled grin.

At lunch that day, Ralph had told me he had mentioned to Vivian that I was coming and had asked her if she would like to see me. Her response had been, Not particularly. She wanted to know whether he was going to bring me to the house. Tell me if you do, she said. Why? he said. So you can leave? She hadn't needed to reply. *Women are different*. I imagined this was Ralph's way of saying that Vivian still hadn't forgiven me. Perhaps she never would.

'I should have agreed to be your best man,' I told him. 'I should have said yes. I still feel bad about that.' I turned to him. 'I'm sorry.'

He gave me another of his sideways glances, more quizzical this time, as if trying to gauge what I was up to.

'Really,' I said. 'I am.'

'At least you came to the wedding.' He stood aside to let an old woman past. 'Do you remember what you gave us?'

'No.'

'A family bible. We thought that was strange.'

I shrugged. 'I suppose we felt like we didn't know you any more. All we knew was, you'd become a Catholic.' Though we had probably thought it was funny too. *Become a Catholic, have you? All right, then. Here's a bible.*

At the time, I told him, I'd had no idea where they were living. I had seen them as a version of Bonnie and Clyde – not just in love, but bound up in each other to such an extent that it removed them from society.

They hadn't wanted *anybody* to know where they were living, Ralph said. Once, they had invited a friend to dinner. They refused to give him their address, though. Instead, they met him in a pub and blindfolded him, only allowing him to see again when he was inside their flat.

I asked Ralph if he blindfolded everyone who came round.

'We wanted our own life,' he said, 'with no one interfering.'

'That's what I thought.'

'I mean, I like you – and I like Robin. It's just that I like Vivian more.'

I fell silent. It seemed that Ralph had got as close to explaining our estrangement as it was possible to get.

By ten o'clock that night, we were in a taxi again, heading back into the centre of Pudong.

'So you didn't have sex with Robin?' Ralph said.

I looked at him. 'No.'

He held my gaze.

The thought of having sex with Robin had never even entered my head. It was a difficult idea to get across, though, especially to somebody so sceptical: I would sound defensive, if not actually guilty, no matter what I said.

I tried another tack. 'Look, I'd tell you if I had,' I said. 'I'm not trying to hide anything. It's not like I'd be embarrassed, or ashamed.'

He looked away finally, but didn't seem convinced.

A few minutes later, he stopped the taxi, saying there was something he wanted to show me. We walked to the next junction. On the corner was a modern office block, neat hedges framing silver revolving doors. Ralph pointed at a spot on the pavement, midway between the building's entrance and the kerb.

'I slept there once,' he said.

Last summer, he had been out by himself, and it had got late. Vivian was in England, visiting family. He was beginning to think he would call it a night when he saw three Chinese men sleeping in a row on the pavement. They looked so comfortable that he lay down beside them. When he woke up, it was raining, and the Chinese men had gone. He was lying on his back on the street, with people stepping all around him.

I smiled. We crossed the road, walking more slowly now. For a while neither of us spoke. The traffic lights changed from red to green, but since there were no cars waiting, nothing happened.

I asked him how he had reacted when Dad died.

'I remember that,' he said.

Vivian had phoned him at work, asking him to come home. He knew from her voice that it was important. When he got back to the flat – they lived in South London then, in Grove Park – she sat him down and told him the news. He cried for about fifteen minutes, and that was it. He didn't cry again. Hands in his pockets, he stared down at his shoes. 'I liked Goat. Goat was all right.' He lifted his eyes again and looked back along the road. 'There's nothing much here, is there?' Hailing a passing taxi, he told me we would have a proper night on Friday. He would show me his Shanghai. We could also meet on Thursday if I liked, for lunch.

It was almost eleven by the time I reached my hotel, and I was hungry, but I didn't feel like going out again. Instead, I walked into the Dream Café on the first floor where a young woman in a black evening gown was seated at a grand piano. Her fine, sleek hair outlined her head so faithfully that I could make out the exact shape of her skull; I could almost feel the tender curve of it against my palm. Apart from the pianist and two chatting waitresses, there was no one else about. I approached the counter and pointed at a sandwich and a can of Singtao beer, then I occupied a table to the left of the piano. From where I was sitting, I couldn't see the young woman's face, only her fingers as they drifted over the keys. She took tunes like 'Come Fly with Me' and 'I've Got You under My Skin', which, given the surroundings, were incongruous enough already, and played them with such a halting, melancholy touch that they became laments. Between numbers, she didn't move from the piano, but sat quite motionless and upright, her hands gripping the leading edge of the stool, her hair falling sheer to the small of her back, and turning dark brown at the ends, like a black cat's fur in the sun.

That night, as I sat in my room on the seventh floor, looking out over the misty, neon-tinted city, I thought how unlikely it was that one tactless remark from Tina, a girl I hadn't lived with in more than a quarter of a century, could trigger such a long estrangement. After leaving the house in Eastbourne in September 1984, I had moved up to London, and Tina and I had started seeing each other again, just as I had suspected we might, but we'd both known that it couldn't last, and the knowledge gave those weeks a beautiful, aching quality, an inbuilt nostalgia, like walking ankle deep in autumn leaves. I still wasn't sure what to do about Hanne. Somehow I couldn't imagine going back to her.

Tina and I split up just before Christmas, and I flew to New York with no plans to return for at least a year. The following February, when Hanne rang me, asking if she could visit – the first anniversary of my father's death was also, of course, her thirty-second birthday – I told her that I didn't think it would work. Not long afterwards, she wrote me a letter saying that she wouldn't try and hold me back; if I wanted to be free, I should be free. She had behaved with such grace that I was humbled. Some months later, I heard that Tina had a new boyfriend. This seemed part of the same pattern.

I was on a different path, a path that would lead to Tokyo, Sydney and Los Angeles, and then, in the autumn of 1988, to a flat in West London and a blonde girl in a plum-coloured rubber dress. Her wide green eyes looked clear through me, as if to a different dimension, her intelligence was fierce and instinctive, and her lips burned the first time she kissed me, on a dark windswept pavement near Portobello Road, so much so that I thought she might be carrying a fever, though she didn't seem ill, not even remotely. Her face was pure and pale and rare, like something that needed looking after, and I thought, I'll look after it, and I knew she would let me. What I didn't know was that we would stay together, and that we would get married, and that there would be, eventually, a miraculous daughter.

Neither my wife nor my daughter had ever seen Ralph. For my daughter, especially, Ralph was a ghost figure, a kind of rumour: she would laugh gaily at the mention of his name, as though I were talking about someone imaginary, someone she didn't quite believe in. I wondered if, in years to come, she would meet him, as I had once met my Uncle Joe. I wondered what he would say to her.

*

With Ralph busy on Tuesday and Wednesday, I explored Shanghai. I stood in the People's Park at dawn and watched an old man in blue silk pyjamas walking backwards, holding a transistor radio. I ate steamed crocodile soup with gastrodia tuber in the house where J. G. Ballard used to live. I found a stationery shop on Fuzhou that sold exquisite handmade paper. I came down with a cold. Though exhausted, I couldn't seem to sleep for more than four hours at a stretch. Some mornings I left my hotel so early that I heard alarm clocks going off as I wandered the empty streets. I was seeing everything off-kilter, through a haze.

When I called Ralph on Thursday to confirm our lunch, he told me that he, too, had been having trouble sleeping. Only the night before, he had dreamt a wild animal was loose in his garden.

'That'll be me, then,' I said.

We both laughed uncertainly, not sure whether such a joke could be made.

I reached his office just after twelve. My suitcase had arrived at last, and I had Ralph's presents with me. As we crossed the drop-off area outside his building, a taxi honked at us.

Ralph's head swivelled. 'All *right*,' he shouted in English. '*Yes*.'

He wasn't angry, or even annoyed. But, like a character in a pantomime, he engaged directly with everything around him. He *responded* to everything. Kate had thought Ralph looked as if he might not have too long to live, but what Frank's photos had failed to show was how alert, how vigorous, how humorously combative he was, so much so that sometimes, as in a cartoon, I imagined I could see a set of curving lines in the air to one side of his head, or his shoulder, or his elbow. He might get himself into altercations, even fights, but he didn't seem like somebody who would die in the near future, and I was glad about that.

The restaurant he took me to – Xin Ji Shi – was airier and more modern than the place we had eaten in on Monday. Once we had a table, and Ralph had ordered drinks, I produced two silver packages from my bag and slid them towards him.

He looked disconcerted, almost indignant. 'What's this? I haven't got *you* anything.'

'You were supposed to have them on Monday,' I said.

Watching him unwrap the smaller of the two presents, I saw that he had his own particular technique. He didn't tear the wrapping, as most people did. Instead, he peeled off the strips of Sellotape, one by one, then painstakingly unrolled the present out of its paper.

The first package contained some Spanish Lucky Strikes.

'Excellent,' he said. 'I'll smoke these next.'

The second present was a book. In a recent e-mail, Ralph had told me that he missed nature, and that the nearest countryside to Shanghai was two hours away by plane. With that in mind, I had bought him *The Wild Places* by Robert Macfarlane, a choice I was even more happy with now I had discovered that Ralph, like the author, had a predilection for sleeping in the open air.

Ralph thanked me for the presents and put them carefully to one side, then he signalled to a waiter and ordered more beer. A discussion began, and it was a while before the waiter walked away and Ralph was able to translate. He had asked the waiter for two new beers, he told me, but the waiter thought he was ordering two *new* beers –

that Ralph wanted a different *make* of beer, in other words – and it had taken Ralph three or four attempts to explain that he wanted two new beers, as in two *more* of the beers he'd ordered *previously*. I was beginning to think that he deliberately provoked these little flurries of misunderstanding. He seemed to feed off the confusion that flourished in the gap between the two cultures.

While Ralph and the waiter had been talking, I had been thinking about Monday night, and how, at one point, we had touched on the subject of the perfect murder. We had agreed that there were moments when an ideal opportunity seems to present itself. I had given Ralph an example from my own life – a chance encounter with two Esperanto speakers on an isolated beach in north-east Brazil. Ralph had listened, nodding, and then described a journey through Portugal in 1982. It was the height of summer, he told me, and the doors of the train had been left open so as to allow air to circulate. Outside, the landscape was barren, empty, just treeless hills and rocks and dried-up riverbeds. There was no one in their carriage apart from a hippie backpacker. At that time, he and Vivian had a private language, Ralph said – they still did, in fact – and they could often have whole conversations without so much as opening their mouths. It occurred to them, looking at each other, that they had taken an instant and violent dislike to the backpacker. It also occurred to them that, since they both had knives on them, they could easily get rid of him. I asked Ralph if they were carrying flick knives, as they had in Eastbourne. No, these were different, he said. Short, curved blades. Probably used for harvesting grapes. In any case. They would attack the hippie, then push him from the moving train. By the time his body was found, they would be in another country –

Spain, or Morocco. There would be no witnesses, and no motive. Nothing to link them to the crime. But you didn't do it, I said to him. We discussed it for half an hour, he said, but in the end we thought, Best not.

Now, all of a sudden, I had a question for Ralph, and it wasn't one that appeared on my list. In fact, it wasn't one I'd thought of before.

'When we were in Eastbourne,' I said slowly, 'did you ever think about killing me and Robin?'

He glanced down at the table, smiling.

'You did, didn't you?' I said.

'Oh yes,' he said. 'For about a week.'

I laughed despite myself. 'How were you going to do it?'

He watched me through his cigarette smoke, head at a jaunty angle. 'You remember the Rover Robin bought?'

I nodded.

'We were going to doctor the brakes,' he said.

They would make it look as if the brake cable had frayed or snapped. It was the kind of thing that happened, wasn't it, in old cars? Thinking of how the gear lever had come away in Robin's hand, I nodded again. They would suggest a joint outing to Beachy Head, Ralph went on, a place Robin and I seemed fond of. Once on the cliff top, though, he and Vivian would announce that they felt like stretching their legs, and they would walk back down, leaving us to drive . . .

'And there's that steep hill,' I said. 'Lorries were always going out of control when we were young and knocking down the wall at the top of our road –'

'It's a one-in-seven gradient,' Ralph said.

I imagined the scenario – Robin stamping on the brake pedal, and the Rover gathering momentum. *They don't make them like they used to.*

'It's not exactly foolproof,' I said. 'I mean, it might not have worked . . .'

'No.' Ralph looked at me and smiled again.

The food came: pork belly in a deep black pot – *hong-shao rou* – winter bamboo green vegetables, and sticky red dates.

'The pork's very good here,' Ralph said.

Obviously, he and Vivian had found it hard living in the house with us, I said, but they seemed to have arrived with preconceived notions. Why else would they have had a Chubb lock fitted on their door right at the beginning?

They'd had the lock fitted, Ralph said, because Robin and I had walked in on Vivian when she was asleep in bed. We had poked around in their private things. Made all sorts of derogatory remarks.

I found myself staring at Ralph again.

'Don't tell me you don't remember,' he said.

As he spoke, I had a vision of Robin in Paradise. He was wearing his overcoat, and hunched over furtively in the corner by the clothes cupboard. I saw him send a sharp glance to his left. Christ, he hissed, she's in here. *Quick!* He meant we should leave the room – though by then, of course, it was already too late.

I shook my head. 'Were we drunk?'

'I don't know. It happened during the day, while I was at work. We only had the lock fitted after that.' Ralph poured the last of the beer into our glasses, then put the empty bottle down. 'You ask this time.' He told me the Chinese for 'beer'.

'Vivian really hated being in that house,' he went on when the waiter had gone. 'You kept drugs in the larder, next to our food. We didn't do drugs. And we couldn't stand those friends of yours who were always hanging round. Graham, and Toby. And that doctor – I've forgotten his name.'

'So how come you were there,' I said, 'if it was all so difficult?'

'I don't know. It seemed the right thing to do at the time.' He lit a Shanghai Gold. 'I probably shouldn't have put her through it.'

I helped myself to more *hongshao rou*, then I brought up the story Dad had told me about Ralph breaking into the house in the middle of the night. Was that true?

'Yes, I think so,' he said.

He had ridden down to Eastbourne with Vivian, but Dad disapproved of her so strongly that he'd had to smuggle her into the house. Climbing on to the roof of the coal shed, he had forced the box-room window and let Vivian in through the back door. They had gone to bed in Robin's old room. Vivian had crept out of the house at dawn and walked down to the seafront. After spending a few hours with Dad, Ralph went to look for her. They hadn't agreed on a meeting-place, and no one had mobiles in those days, but he didn't have too much trouble finding her. She was the only girl asleep on the beach.

'Did you ever take things from the house?' I asked. 'Dad thought you were taking things.'

'I don't remember taking anything.' Ralph looked straight at me. 'There wasn't much to take, was there?'

Our last encounter was on Friday evening. We had agreed that Ralph should meet me at my hotel at half past six. By ten to seven, though, he still hadn't shown up. When I opened the door of my room and peered out, he was standing by the lift in his long black raincoat, a mobile pressed to his left ear. He had forgotten my room number, he said, and was just calling reception. I told him to come in, but he held up his hands, palms facing outwards.

'It's your room,' he said. 'Private.'

'It's a hotel room,' I said. 'And anyway, I'm not like you. It doesn't bother me.'

'All right.'

Once through the door, his head twisted on his neck, his eyes darting this way and that, his nose seeming to ferret at the air. He wore the same clothes he had worn on Monday night, and when he came and stood next to me, bending over a detailed map of Shanghai so as to point out the location of the village we had visited, he gave off a musty, almost feral smell. I was struck by how perfectly it went with his behaviour.

Ten minutes later, we were hailing a taxi outside my hotel. Ralph told the driver we were looking for a restaurant that served duck. The driver said he knew of one nearby. As we edged eastwards on Huaihai Lu, with its delicate arches of white neon and its crowds of window-shoppers, a black car drew alongside us. A well-groomed Chinese woman sat behind the wheel. When she glanced in our direction, Ralph waved at her. I expected her to ignore him, but she smiled and waved back.

'You like strangers, don't you?' I said.

'Those moments with people you don't know,' he said, his head against the headrest, his voice subdued, almost dreamy, 'those chance connections, they can lift your heart a little . . .'

In the *Shanghai Daily News* that morning, I had read an article about *otaku*, a Japanese term that referred to people who lived their lives at one remove, online. A junior lecturer at Shanghai University was reported as saying that the 'smell of crowds' gave him a headache. 'When I see strangers,' he went on, 'I try to treat them as part of the neutral architecture.' Ralph was the opposite. He wanted continual interaction, even if it was fleeting. *Especially* if it was fleeting. Walk down every alley, he had told me on Monday. Look in every doorway. They don't mind.

The restaurant our taxi driver had recommended was huge and bustling, and we were seated on a kind of dais, next to a window that ran the entire length of the room. From our table, we could look down into Huaihai Lu, the splashes of mauve and crimson neon making the street seem painted.

'I'm sorry to go on about it,' I said when our drinks had arrived, 'but I still don't understand what happened – why we lost touch so completely.'

I reminded him of what he had said when we last spoke, in 1987. *Don't phone me again. If you want to contact me, do it in writing.*

'You took me very literally,' Ralph said quietly.

'What did you expect?' I said.

Ralph lit a cigarette. His face had taken on a strange, blurred expression, as if a long estrangement wasn't something he had ever intended or envisaged, and not before time, perhaps, I saw my own part in it quite clearly. I had always assumed that it was Ralph who had severed ties with the family. Was I really all that different, though? I had felt so put upon, so *commandeered*, that I had needed, once I had the chance, to get away – as far away as possible. All those places I had lived in: Athens, Berlin, New York, Tokyo, Los Angeles, Sydney, Amsterdam, Rome . . . The list went on and on. That couldn't *just* be curiosity, could it? I remembered watching Ralph and his wife and daughter from Dad's bedroom window on that perfect summer's day in 1984 and thinking how fragile they looked – but a family could be predatory too. *Families are the beginning of destruction*, as the Chinese poet, Gu Cheng, put it – and then there was Sonya's telling use of the word 'separated' . . . I was still pondering the degree to which I had cut myself off from the family when Ralph spoke again, and it was immediately apparent that he had been following a different line of thought entirely.

'What's the worst thing you ever said?' he asked.

I talked about having lied to Dad when I last saw him. Ralph agreed that this was pretty unforgivable, then asked if I remembered the piece of hardboard Dad used to lean on when he was writing or drawing. I said I did. Once, he had been cheeky to Dad, he said, and when Dad made as though to swipe him with the hardboard he'd told Dad not to be so pathetic.

'I called him pathetic,' Ralph said.

I winced. 'What did he do?'

'He didn't do anything. He just sort of stared off into the top corner of the room.'

'I know that look.'

'I shouldn't have said it. It was cruel.' Ralph dragged on his cigarette, then looked down into the street.

'I think he did his best,' I said. 'I know he loved us. It can't have been easy.'

I told Ralph something Beth had told me when I saw her last. On the day of our mother's funeral, Beth had come across Dad and Ralph in what was then the dining-room. Ralph was standing on a chair, and Dad was beside him with his arm round Ralph's shoulders, and the two of them were staring at the wreaths laid out on the drive.

'It was still gravel then, wasn't it?' Ralph said.

I nodded, watching him.

He put out his cigarette. 'If I could bring one person back, it would be her.'

'Me too,' I said.

Later, as we crossed Suzhou Creek, our taxi heading for a run-down area near the north end of the Yangpu bridge, I decided not to ask any more questions. From now on, we were just two brothers, out for the night.

We pulled up outside the Live Bar, which was where Ralph had played trumpet when he first moved to Shanghai, and which was hosting what it called a 'winter punkers' Assembly!'. Once a warehouse, the club had a stark industrial atmosphere, with a concrete floor and plenty of metallic surfaces. It was so cold that I kept my coat on. We watched as four girls in stylish black outfits took the stage and made as much noise as they could. When I turned and grinned at Ralph, he mouthed the words, *Aren't they sweet?* We drank two beers, then went to a karaoke bar further down the street. 'It looks like there's nothing here, doesn't it?' he said as I followed him up a steep flight of wooden stairs between two buildings. He led me into a brown room. Green plastic foliage coiled on the ceiling. There was a small TV on the bar, and a larger one fixed high up in the corner. It was even colder than the last place. We were the only foreigners.

'They want me to sing,' Ralph said when he returned with our drinks.

The woman who ran the bar handed him a cordless mike. He moved towards the smaller of the two TVs and began to sing in Chinese. His voice was young and clear, and so unforced that it sounded almost casual. Since he was facing away from me, I could only see his long black coat, the back of his head, and the lit cigarette in his left hand, but once, halfway through the first song, he turned and gestured in my direction, and even though I couldn't understand the words, I felt nothing but good coming from him.

If he could bring one person back, he had said, it would be our mother. And I had agreed. Because that, I realized, was what I had been trying to do. I had been visiting people who used to know her. Asking questions. Filling in the empty spaces. And I had glimpses of her now, the woman who danced around the room with no clothes on when my father asked her to marry him, the woman who hugged me tight against her in the cold, the woman who was so enthusiastic, and so cheerful, and so afraid of growing old. My darling. All my life I had been haunted by her absence. Haunted by her failure to return. Her shadow lay across me like a fall of snow. But now I had learned enough, perhaps, to free myself from that exquisite, paralysing chill, that weight. Now, at last, I could bury her.

When Ralph had sung two numbers, he gave the microphone back and sat down. The bar filled with loud applause.

I put a hand on his shoulder. 'That was brilliant. Were you reading the Chinese?'

'Only for the second song.' The first – 'Moonlight Represents My Heart' – was a song that everybody in China knew, he said, and one that he'd been taught when he arrived.

A group of Chinese men strolled in and rearranged tables and chairs in such a way that they occupied the centre of the room. The ringleader had a face that shone, as if it had been greased, and his neck was thick, like a wrestler's. He wore an iridescent emerald-green shell-suit top with the word BRAZIL emblazoned across the shoulder blades in yellow.

I leaned close to Ralph. 'I don't like the look of them.'

'They're probably gangsters,' he said.

The man in the green top raised his glass to us, then drained it. Ralph did the same.

'You'd better drink as well,' he muttered. 'You have to empty your glass, or it's an insult.'

I finished my beer.

Later, a thin, stooping gangster picked up the mike and began to sing. His suit was the drab grey of the fluff that collects in tumble dryers.

'He's *dreadful*,' I whispered.

Ralph thought it might be best to go. If they asked us to join them, we wouldn't be able to say no, and then we'd never get away. As we left the bar we shook hands with the man in the green jacket, and he gave us a broad smile whose meaning I couldn't gauge.

Out on the pavement again, Ralph suggested a foot massage. We walked back along the street and pushed through a plate-glass door. Inside, two women were watching car crashes on TV. Betty was tall and mannish, with long black hair and tight-fitting dark blue jeans. Janet had a dumpier physique. She wore a denim miniskirt and a pale blue synthetic top with a scoop neck, and her hair, which was short and frizzy, was dyed a strange brown colour, like burnt sugar. Against the left-hand wall stood a row of lumpy armchairs, each one covered with a large bright orange towel. In front of the chairs were buckets lined with blue plastic bags.

Ralph studied the price list on the wall. 'There's a whole range of services on offer.'

'You said feet.'

He grinned. 'That's twenty yuan.'

I sat down next to Ralph, and Janet settled on a low stool in front of me. She took off my shoes and socks, then rolled up my trouser-legs and lifted both my feet into the plastic bucket, which she had filled with warm water. When she had washed and dried my feet, she rested them on her knees and began to massage them, starting with the toes. Her fingers were strong, seeming to reach between the bones.

After a while, she said something that made Ralph laugh.

'She doesn't believe we're brothers,' he told me.

I asked why not.

'Because my legs are white and yours are yellow.'

Janet leaned forwards, her breasts touching my shins. She looked into my face, then spoke to Ralph. 'She says you have beautiful eyes,' he said, translating. 'They're blue.'

'They're not blue,' I said. 'They're more sort of grey-green – like that cushion over there.'

Now I leaned forwards, which made Janet giggle. 'She has beautiful eyes as well,' I said. 'They're brown.'

Ralph translated.

'She says they're black,' he said.

Janet spoke again.

'She wants to shag you.' Ralph tilted his head in the rough direction of a flimsy chipboard partition. 'There's probably a little room in the back.' He was grinning again. 'She says it wouldn't take long.'

'I'm not sure that's a good idea,' I said.

Ralph explained to Janet that I was expected some-where else. As she listened to him, she pushed her hands up past my knees, her fingers gripping the muscles in my lower thighs.

On TV the car crashes had become more extreme. Now they were showing footage of a pile-up on a motorway.

'Not very relaxing,' Ralph said.

When Janet spoke again, she kept her eyes on me, their corners narrowing with mischief.

I turned to Ralph. 'What's she saying now?'

'She's wondering which hotel you're staying at.' His massage over, Ralph started pulling on his socks. 'She doesn't want you to go. She loves you.'

'You could be making this up for all I know.'

Still bending down, doing up a shoe, Ralph smiled. 'Yes, I suppose that's true.'

When I got to my feet, Janet wrapped her arms around my waist and laid her head sideways against my chest. She suddenly seemed much younger, like an affectionate but slightly wilful child.

By the time we left the massage parlour, it was half past eleven, and the bands in the Live Bar had finished playing. We set off down a narrow, poorly lit street called Tongbei Lu, in search of a pool table.

'My feet feel better than they did before,' I told Ralph. 'More alive, somehow.'

As I spoke, a pretty girl with an oddly disjointed walk fell into step with us. She asked what we were looking for, then offered to take us to a place she knew. I thought she was trying to be helpful, but Ralph wasn't convinced. There was usually some kind of scam going on, he said. Probably she had an arrangement with a local bar, and would be paid ten yuan for every Westerner she brought in. He felt we would be wasting our time if we went with her – unless, of course, I wanted to. I shook my head.

When Ralph told her we had decided to take a taxi to Pudong, she seemed surprised, though not particularly disappointed. As she moved awkwardly away through the dim ochre light, I had the impression that her body was only being held together by her clothes. She was like a packet of biscuits that had been dropped: it looks whole while the wrapper's on, but when you open it everything's in pieces.

Ralph knew of three bars, which were all on the same stretch of road. In the first, he bought two Coronas. While we were waiting to play pool, a girl in a red satin blouse walked over. She was called Swallow. She told us foreigners were always laughing at her name. We said it was a lovely name. Poetic. I told her about Rome in the autumn, and how, at dusk, the air was full of swallows, and how agile they seemed, and how decisive. But if she didn't like the foreigners laughing, she might consider changing her name to Raven, I said, on account of her black hair, or even Wren, since she was so petite. On the pool table, a Chinese man in his early twenties was winning game after game. His hair hung in glamorous spikes over his eyes. Ralph had seen him play before and didn't think we had much chance of beating him.

After we had both lost, we said goodbye to Swallow and moved on to the next bar. It was closed. The third bar was further down, the scarlet of its neon fuzzy and soft-focus in the fog. We pushed through the door. Low lighting, smoky air. Girls' faces floating up out of the gloom. I met Pamela, who had wide, almost Mongolian cheekbones and chaotically backcombed hair. She wore a shiny black plastic jacket with pointy lapels and black-and-white hooped leg warmers. Pamela introduced us to Fei Xu, whose hair was long and straight with tawny highlights.

She was dressed more conventionally, in a pale-pink T-shirt and jeans.

Ralph ordered a round of drinks – Corona for us, Malibu for them. I went to the bathroom. Above the urinal, three small muddy paintings hung in an uneven row. Back in the bar, Ralph was talking to a brawny American called Kurt or Dwayne. There's art in the toilet, I said. What's it like? Ralph said. Brown, I said. He laughed. No, really, I said. Pamela had rested her head sideways on the bar, her face turned towards us. She said she was sleepy. She needed another Malibu. You haven't finished the last one yet, Ralph said. He told me that she would probably have been in the bar since about midday.

We bought more drinks and then played pool, Ralph and Pamela against me and Fei Xu. I lost all sense of time, but it didn't bother me how late it got. I was with my brother; there was nowhere I would rather be.

Every once in a while, between rounds, we would order shots of vodka. The girls wanted vodka too. We tried to persuade Pamela to have tonic with it – we didn't want her to get too drunk – but she howled in protest, sounding, for a moment, exactly like a cat.

At six in the morning, we asked if we could settle up. Our tab came to 615 yuan, or more than £40, and we barely had enough money between us. I hugged Pamela goodbye. She was so tiny that she nearly got lost in the folds of my coat.

Out on the street, in the cold, Ralph and I stood facing in different directions. His bar was great, I said. It had made me feel like Alice in Wonderland. He grinned. As he began to tell me that he should be going home, his mobile rang. He put it to his ear.

'What are *you* doing awake?' he said.

I knew then that Vivian was on the other end.

'No, it's been fine,' he said. 'It's been lovely.'

I had come to China to see Ralph. All the same, it felt strange to have Vivian's voice so close, and to know that she would have nothing to do with me. Was what had happened in 1984 so terrible that not even twenty-three years were enough to wipe it out? A wave of regret swept through me, and I walked a few paces up the street.

'I'll be back in a minute,' I heard Ralph say. 'I just need to get some money.'

Cars surged, one by one, through air that was dense and sluggish. Soon it would be light.

Turning, I saw Ralph slide his mobile into his pocket.

'Vivian,' he said.

We caught a taxi to the nearest ATM machine, and I watched as Ralph ran across an intersection, then hunched over the metal key-pad, punching buttons. These were our last seconds. He climbed back into the taxi and handed me two red 100-yuan notes. 'You paid for almost everything back there.' We hugged briefly, then he got out and shut the door. As the taxi pulled away, I turned and peered through the back window. Ralph was walking at the edge of the wide road in his black coat, his face already indistinct, almost featureless, and because the taxi was moving faster than he was, because he was diminishing so rapidly, he appeared to be travelling in the opposite direction, away from me. The feeling that went through me in that moment was so fierce and unalloyed that it took me back to adolescence. Though we had only just parted, I already longed to see him again. Would he be feeling something similar? I doubted it. Probably he would be thinking of getting home – his wife still awake, his daughter stirring . . .

It was eight o'clock when I climbed into bed. Despite the Do Not Disturb light outside my room, the maids kept trying my door, especially around midday. I slept fitfully until three in the afternoon. On getting up, my first instinct was to call Ralph. I resisted, though; I had bothered him enough. Every now and then, I would glance at the phone, but I didn't pick up the receiver.

On Sunday morning, I flew back to London.

You took me very literally. That sentence of Ralph's had stayed with me. There was a ruefulness about it, but at the same time he could almost have been reproaching me. Perhaps I should have reacted differently. Ignored what he was saying, or even told him not to be silly. Like a Chinese taxi driver, though, I had been baffled, even paralysed, by Ralph's directions. He seemed surprised that we'd had so little to do with each other, but not unduly upset. In the context of his life, I wasn't that important. All he needed was his family – the one he had made – and a handful of strangers, people he came across by chance and drank with, or joked about, or waved at from car windows. *I mean, I like you – and I like Robin. It's just that I like Vivian more.*

Still, I was happy to have seen him. I had put things that had been troubling me into words. I had said I was sorry. And I had received answers to questions I hadn't even asked. It hadn't been in my mind, for instance, to wonder what I felt for Ralph, but I had found out on Saturday as the distance opened up between us, as he was swallowed by the murky grey-brown of a Shanghai dawn. Love had caught me unawares, reaching out through the back window of the taxi like a line thrown from my heart. Because he seemed to be sinking – a leaf in water. Because I seemed to be losing him again. This love was strong – no, unconditional – and he could do whatever he wanted with it. Even nothing. Nothing was fine. But I would be there for him if he ever needed me. He could call on me. Rely on me. There would be no more letters saying no.

The Burning Bed

On our last morning in the house, it's the hammering of my heart that wakes me. I am lying on the carpet, in a sleeping-bag. I feel as if I have overslept, and am now late for an appointment. Panic swarms through me, but still I don't move. The house sounds hollow, like the inside of a cello. In the kitchen, a loose piece of parquet lifts under someone's foot, then clacks back into place. The others are already up.

I imagine the house might have felt like this thirty-five years ago, when my grandmother left for the asylum. There would have been the same unnatural quiet, the same air of imminent abandonment. Who kept an eye on things after she was gone? Did anyone? I wonder if local children thought of the house as haunted. *A mad lady lived here once. She had funny teeth. Her hair turned white in an earthquake.*

When my parents arrived in the early 1950s, the dust was half an inch thick, and dead flies lay in brittle, glinting heaps on all the windowsills. My mother had to scrub every surface with detergent, then there was the decorating to be done. You should have seen it, my father told me once. The whole place was *brown*. Wendy had spent most of her childhood in the house. She had only been away for three or four years. How did she feel about returning? Had she imagined a different, more exotic life?

A door slams downstairs.

I glance at my alarm clock. Ten to ten. Unzipping my sleeping-bag, I scramble to my feet.

Since the kitchen table and the chairs have been destroyed, we have to eat breakfast standing up. Afterwards we throw everything into the skip – kettle, teapot, mugs and plates, the cutlery. By a quarter to twelve, we are ready to leave. Ralph and Vivian have ordered a taxi to take them to the station. They are renting a place in Scauri, not far from Naples. They have no idea how long they will be away, or where they will be living when they come back. Robin and I will drive up to London in the Rover. To start with, we'll stay in the Oval. Robin plans to buy a flat of his own with his share of the proceeds from the house. I will go and see Hanne in West Berlin, then I'm thinking of spending a few months in New York. I will keep in touch with Robin, as I always have, but I can't imagine when I'll next see Ralph.

We gather in the hall, uncertain what to say now that our time together is over. Then Robin lets out a gasp.

'My bed,' he says.

We have forgotten about Dad's bed. If it's in the house at midday, it will constitute a breach of the agreement, and the sale might fall through. We all start talking at once. *The skip! What about the skip? No, wait. The skip's already full.* We only have one option: the bonfire.

We rush upstairs and into Dad's bedroom. Judging by the pale, hazy air above the hedge, the fire's still just about alight. We upend the mattress. Slide it out of the room. Once outside, we lay it flat, then drag it up the garden and hurl it on to the remains of last night's blaze. We race back to the house. The base proves more unwieldy. Even flipped on to its side, it barely fits through Dad's bedroom doorway. On the landing, we have to lift it above our heads so as to manoeuvre it down the stairs. We knock against a banister post; it creaks, but doesn't break. By the time we reach the kitchen garden, blue-grey smoke is seeping from beneath the mattress. We heave the base on to the mattress, but it slips sideways, ending up on the scorched ground that surrounds the fire. We should have put the base on first; with its wooden frame, it would have burned more easily. Swearing, we take a corner each and hoist it skywards, then lower it again. This time it stays put, its four stumpy black legs sticking up in the air, its hairy hessian belly shamelessly exposed.

From the road comes the sound of a car's horn. Ralph's taxi. The three of us run down the garden. Ralph disappears through the French window, but Robin and I stop outside the glasshouse. We're breathing through our mouths, like animals.

'Look,' I say, pointing at the hedge.

The smoke flooding up into the sky has changed colour: it is darker now, and oilier.

Robin nods grimly. 'Another helicopter.'

I watch as one final suitcase is wedged into the taxi's boot. Ralph and Vivian have an unbelievable amount of luggage; I'm not sure how they're going to carry it all. Along with the clothes and baby things, Ralph has packed his trumpet and a set of Dickens novels. He is also taking some of Dad's tools – the hand-drill, the axe and several balls of string – which he thinks will come in useful in Italy. Vivian is already sitting in the taxi. Her long hair screens her face. I still don't understand what came between us. There were nights when we got on, but the next day the awkwardness and tension would be back. Perhaps we're not supposed to be close, or even to know each other at all. We're not exactly the first family to fray around the edges. Life tends to unravel, given half a chance. Some loose ends just get looser.

I remember how Ralph and I used to play football together on Christmas Eve. It was a ritual of ours – only the two of us, and only on that one night of the year. The most thrilling of all nights if you're young: the ground quartz-like and crackling with frost, the smell of candle smoke, the multicoloured paper chains looping through the downstairs rooms, the stockings, as yet unfilled, draped limply across our beds . . .

I can see us on the drive, me fifteen, him ten. My turn in goal. I crouch in front of the five-bar gate. To my left, the yew trees, quill-sharp at the top, and inky black. Darkness is falling, but there's still a blue glow to the sky behind the house, a halo of uncanny, spectral light, as though a spaceship has just touched down on the lawn. He places the ball and takes a few steps back. He gives me a crafty look. Darts forward. Shoots. The ball flies past my outstretched hand, over the gate. Luckily, no cars are going by. Standing quite still, we listen as the ball bounces off down the road. Then our eyes meet, and we laugh.